Intelligent Automation Simplified

Learn Enterprise Automation, AI-Led Automation, and Robotic Process Automation with Use-cases

Debanjana Dasgupta

www.bpbonline.com

FIRST EDITION 2022
Copyright © BPB Publications, India
ISBN: 978-93-91392-543

All Rights Reserved. No part of this publication may be reproduced, distributed or transmitted in any form or by any means or stored in a database or retrieval system, without the prior written permission of the publisher with the exception to the program listings which may be entered, stored and executed in a computer system, but they can not be reproduced by the means of publication, photocopy, recording, or by any electronic and mechanical means.

LIMITS OF LIABILITY AND DISCLAIMER OF WARRANTY

The information contained in this book is true to correct and the best of author's and publisher's knowledge. The author has made every effort to ensure the accuracy of these publications, but publisher cannot be held responsible for any loss or damage arising from any information in this book.

All trademarks referred to in the book are acknowledged as properties of their respective owners but BPB Publications cannot guarantee the accuracy of this information.

To View Complete
BPB Publications Catalogue
Scan the QR Code:

www.bpbonline.com

Dedicated to

*Late Dr Tarapada Bhowmik and
Mr Tapan Dasgupta*

*My father-in-law and my father,
the inspirations behind this book.*

About the Author

Debanjana Dasgupta is an experienced IT architect and consultant, who for the past 25 years has been working with customers across the globe, designing various technological solutions to resolve their business problems. She completed her engineering from Jadavpur University, Kolkata majoring in Electrical Engineering and started her career with a leading IT company. In her career, she has worked with several Indian and Global IT majors, serving plethora of global clients across industries. She is currently employed with a leading MNC and focused on Intelligent Automation. She is based out of Delhi, India.

Apart from her job, Debanjana loves to coach, mentor, and teach and is actively involved in mentoring IT architects and technical professionals in her organization and beyond.

Outside work, she is an avid traveler and a passionate musician.

About the Reviewer

Dr. Soumya Sankar Basu has over 25 years of experience in academics and software services and consulting industry. He currently serves as a Senior Lecturer of Software Engineering and Computer Science in Department of Computing, Sheffield Hallam University, Sheffield, United Kingdom. Prior to joining university, he worked for tier 1 software services and consulting organizations like IBM Global Business Services, PricewaterhouseCoopers Consulting, Wipro Technologies.

Dr. Basu is a Ph.D (Engineering) from department of Computer Science and Engineering, Jadavpur University, India. Prior to that he has have a master's in computer applications, and bachelor's with honours in Mathematics. After joining academia for full time, he has done a post graduate certificate in higher education and has earned Fellowship of UK Higher Education Academy.

His current research interest is in Global Software Engineering, Software Engineering Methodologies, Software Architecture, Internet of Things, Mobile Ad-hoc and Sensor Networks. His specialization as an industry professional lies in Software Architecture, Application Architecture, Software Engineering Governance, Software Engineering, Process Method Tools, Software Development Methodologies (including Agile/DevOps/Garage method), Design Thinking, Requirement Engineering, Object Oriented Programming Cloud Based Application Development, Cognitive Dynamic Automation, Robotic Process Automation, RFID Application Development and Internet of Things.

He is actively involved in industry consulting in cloud and IoT area. Right now, he is teaching Software Design, Contemporary Software Engineering, Object Oriented Programming and Distributed Programming. In past he taught courses on Architectural Thinking, Design Thinking, Software Development Methodology (Agile/DevOps/Garage), etc.

He publishes papers in journals and refereed conferences. And has authored a book chapter. He has significant work around Software Engineering and Application Architecture area. Because of company confidentiality reason, they had to be published in company internal prestigious forums.

Dr. Basu is currently living in England. Earlier he has worked in multicultural environment with people from across the globe and lived in ASEAN, European countries and Canada for his professional engagements.

Acknowledgement

I am blessed to have many people in my life, who have made this book possible. In this journey, there were times, when along with work and home responsibilities, writing this book seemed like a herculean task. I take this opportunity to thank them all.

First and foremost, I would like to thank my husband, Joy Bhowmik and my children, Abhimanyu and Aaratrika, for putting up with me while I was spending weekends and evenings on writing. My children provided constant support and motivation, often chasing me on my deadlines. I could have never completed this book without their support.

My mom, Manisha Dasgupta and my father, Tapan Dasgupta, silently provided the motivation to get this completed. My father-in-law, Late Dr Tarapada Bhowmik and my mother-in-law, Late Mrs Uma Bhowmik ushered their blessings from above and made this real.

This book wouldn't have happened if I hadn't had the support from my workplace and my manager, Amitabha Mitra, who helped me with the corporate IP approval and from whom I have learnt a lot, as we traversed the enterprise automation journey in the corporate world.

Finally, I would like to thank BPB Publications for giving me this opportunity to write my first book for them and my fantastic editors at BPB Publications, for helping me along the way.

And, my readers, hope you enjoy reading this book, as much I enjoyed writing it.

Preface

Intelligent Automation one of the key drivers in business transformation today. It has now become a part of the enterprise strategy of many large organizations. From back-office automation of manual, labor intensive processes, Intelligent Automation now finds a seat in discussions on enterprise transformation, automating customer journeys spanning across front, mid and back offices. It is now one of the key pillars of the digital and process transformation which delivers the promise of adaptive, intelligent, and self-healing processes across the enterprise.

When I started working in Intelligent Automation in around 2015, it was primarily RPA centric. The tools were still maturing, and automation was still to prove its full potential beyond a few back-office operations. Today, it's a different scenario altogether. Industry 4.0 has automation powered by AI as its key lever and discussions on automation are prevalent across all segments and industries today. Intelligent Automation has proved that it is here to stay.

I learnt automation mostly on the job, starting from designing core automation solutions, driving delivery, and deployment to consulting Fortune 500 clients on Intelligent Automation Strategy and transformation. I have been a part of the evolution of automation to Intelligent Automation and soaked in the buzz around it. The idea of this book emerged with the thought to pass on the knowledge and experience I have accumulated over the years, to younger professionals, and help them get a holistic idea about Intelligent Automation from a practical perspective. This book is to help such professionals to implement Intelligent Automation in their respective organizations. It's written in simple language to enable readers, get the essence of Intelligent Automation without sounding too technical about it. I have embedded practical tips and stories from my experience to help readers navigate through real projects in their jobs.

Over the 7 chapters in this book, you will learn the following:

Chapter 1 introduces Intelligent Automation as a concept and how it has evolved. It then focuses on the different levels of automation, the various components on Intelligent Automation and finally touches upon some of the impacts of automation in the context of future of work.

Chapter 2 discusses Robotic Process Automation in detail, with its characteristics and capabilities. It tells you how to decide which use cases are best suited by RPA and how to go about developing them. It touches upon some of the leading products and solutions

Chapter 3 focusses on Artificial Intelligence, what it entails and the various capabilities of AI that are relevant in the context of Intelligent Automation and how to decide which use cases are fit for AI implementation.

Chapter 4 discusses the other technological components that make up Intelligent Automation like BPM, Blockchain, IoT, Integration and best practices for implementing them in the enterprise.

Chapter 5 is the most important chapter of the book. It describes several key use cases across business and IT automation. It describes the processes, tells you how to select the automation levers, how to design the Intelligent Automation solution with the aid of detailed component design diagrams.

Chapter 6 is a key chapter which discusses, in depth, the enterprise automation journey, why we need an Intelligent Automation Center of Excellence and what are the key capabilities of a CoE that can help an enterprise scale automation.

Chapter 7 is the last chapter and before wrapping up, touches upon some of the key trending topics around automation today. Citizen development, Process Mining and AIOps are discussed in detail before ending the chapter with Future of Work – the impact of Intelligent Automation.

Technology is rapidly evolving, and the pandemic has forced all of us to adapt and thrive in the new environment. I am certain, that over the next few years, we will see more evolution of Intelligent Automation as it becomes farther mainstream and touches every aspect of our lives.

Downloading the coloured images:

Please follow the link to download the
Coloured Images of the book:

https://rebrand.ly/311354

Errata

We take immense pride in our work at BPB Publications and follow best practices to ensure the accuracy of our content to provide with an indulging reading experience to our subscribers. Our readers are our mirrors, and we use their inputs to reflect and improve upon human errors, if any, that may have occurred during the publishing processes involved. To let us maintain the quality and help us reach out to any readers who might be having difficulties due to any unforeseen errors, please write to us at :

errata@bpbonline.com

Your support, suggestions and feedbacks are highly appreciated by the BPB Publications' Family.

> Did you know that BPB offers eBook versions of every book published, with PDF and ePub files available? You can upgrade to the eBook version at www.bpbonline.com and as a print book customer, you are entitled to a discount on the eBook copy. Get in touch with us at :
>
> **business@bpbonline.com** for more details.
>
> At **www.bpbonline.com**, you can also read a collection of free technical articles, sign up for a range of free newsletters, and receive exclusive discounts and offers on BPB books and eBooks.

BPB is searching for authors like you

If you're interested in becoming an author for BPB, please visit **www.bpbonline.com** and apply today. We have worked with thousands of developers and tech professionals, just like you, to help them share their insight with the global tech community. You can make a general application, apply for a specific hot topic that we are recruiting an author for, or submit your own idea.

The code bundle for the book is also hosted on GitHub at **https://github.com/bpbpublications/Intelligent-Automation-Simplified**. In case there's an update to the code, it will be updated on the existing GitHub repository.

We also have other code bundles from our rich catalog of books and videos available at **https://github.com/bpbpublications**. Check them out!

PIRACY

If you come across any illegal copies of our works in any form on the internet, we would be grateful if you would provide us with the location address or website name. Please contact us at :
business@bpbonline.com with a link to the material.

If you are interested in becoming an author

If there is a topic that you have expertise in, and you are interested in either writing or contributing to a book, please visit **www.bpbonline.com**.

REVIEWS

Please leave a review. Once you have read and used this book, why not leave a review on the site that you purchased it from? Potential readers can then see and use your unbiased opinion to make purchase decisions, we at BPB can understand what you think about our products, and our authors can see your feedback on their book. Thank you!

For more information about BPB, please visit **www.bpbonline.com**.

Table of Contents

1. **Introduction to Intelligent Automation** 1
   Introduction 1
   Structure 2
   Objective 2
   Introduction to Automation 2
      Evolution of automation in Information Technology 3
      Different Stages of Automation 8
         Basic automation 9
         Intermediate automation 10
         Intelligent Automation 12
         Automation of tasks, activity, and processes 14
      Examples of Intelligent Automation 16
      Intelligent automation technology components 18
         Robotic Process Automation 19
         Fitment of Robotic Process Automation 20
         Artificial Intelligence (AI) 21
         Fitment of AI components for automation 23
         Workflows and Business Process Management 24
         Fitment of workflow for Automation 25
         Business Intelligence 25
         Integration 26
         Virtual Assistants and Chatbots 27
         Blockchain and IoT 28
      Impact of Automation in an Enterprise 29
      Future of Work 30
   Conclusion 31

2. **Robotic Process Automation** 33
   Introduction 33

Structure 34
Objective 34
Purpose of RPA 34
Characteristics of RPA 35
    Key Characteristics *35*
        Rule based *36*
        Non disruptive *36*
    Benefits of Robotic Process Automation *37*
        Employee time savings *38*
        Improved Process Efficiency *38*
        Increased accuracy and reduced human errors *39*
        Better turn around time *39*
        Employees can focus on more strategic tasks *40*
        Consistency *40*
        Reliability *40*
        Audit Trail *41*
        Scalability *41*
    What makes a process fit for Robotic Process Automation ... 42
        Technical Characteristics of Process required for RPA based Automation *42*
        Non-Technical Characteristics of Process required for RPA based Automation *44*
    Applicability of Robotic Process Automation through examples 45
        Financial Crime *46*
        Core Banking *46*
        Finance and Accounting *46*
        Procurement *47*
        Customer/Vendor Management *48*
        Patient Management in Healthcare *48*
        Payroll in HR *49*
        Generic use cases *49*

■ *xiii*

      IT Operations use cases 50

    Preferred practices 51

          Business Case Validation 53

          Delivery Project Planning and Kick off 53

          Environment Preparation 53

      RPA implementation 54

          Monitor and measure 55

      Bot or API 56

      Products and tools 56

          RPA tools 57

    Conclusion 58

    Reference 59

3. Artificial Intelligence in Automation 61

    Introduction 61

    Structure 62

    Objective 62

    Purpose of Artificial Intelligence in Automation 63

    Different types of AI in intelligent automation 64

      Image Recognition 67

          Natural Language Processing 69

          Recommendation and Prediction 70

          Other Machine Learning 71

          Benefits of Artificial Intelligence in Automation 71

      Fitment of Processes for Artificial Intelligence
      based Automation 73

          Technical Characteristics of the Process required for
          AI based Automation 74

          Non-Technical Characteristics of Process required
          for AI based Automation 75

      Applicability of Artificial Intelligence in Automation
      through a few typical use cases 77

　　　　　Financial Services 77
　　　　　Retail 78
　　　　　AI in IT Operations Automation 80
　　　　　Other use cases 81
　　　AI delivery Life cycle 81
　　　　　Use Case Identification and Assessment 83
　　　　　Data Collection and building Dataset 83
　　　　　Train the model 84
　　　　　Refine and Test 84
　　　　　Deploy 85
　　　Products and tools 85
　　　　　Some common Machine Learning Frameworks 86
　　　　　Some common Deep Learning Frameworks 86
　Conclusion 87
　References 88

4. **Other Technologies in Automation** 89
　Introduction 89
　Structure 90
　Objective 90
　Blockchain 90
　　　Fitment of processes for blockchain based automation 93
　　　　　Immutability 93
　　　　　Single source of truth 93
　　　　　Traceable provenance 94
　　　　　Trust 94
　　　Blockchain use cases for Intelligent Automation 95
　　　　　Digital identity and inheritances 95
　　　　Digital identity 95
　　　　Inheritances and Wills 96
　　　　Financial services 96

       Capital markets 96

       Financial record keeping 97

       Logistics 97

  Internet of Things 98

       Characteristics of IoT 99

       Connected devices 99

       Sensing ability 99

       Data acquisition and transfer 100

       Data processing 100

       Scalability 100

       Security 100

  IoT Use cases 100

       What makes a process fit for the IoT implementation in Intelligent Automation? 102

            Fitment of processes for the IoT based Automation 102

            Delivering IoT Projects 103

  Workflow.. 105

       Fitment of processes for Workflow based Automation 106

  Integration 108

       Use cases 109

  Conclusion 111

  References 112

5. Intelligent Automation Use Cases 113

  Introduction...113

  Structure...114

  Objectives...114

  Introduction to the Use cases 114

  Use case in Banking..115

       Use case 1: KYC Processing 116

       Introduction 116

       High-level Process...117

      Detailed process view 118

         Identification of the primary and secondary levers of automation 120

         High-level solution diagram 121

         Detailed internal view of the selected automation components 122

      Use case 2: Automated Service Request/Ticket Creation ... 126

         Introduction 126

         High-level Process 127

         Detailed Process 128

         Identification of the primary and secondary levers of automation 129

         High-level Solution 129

         Detailed internal view of selected automation components ...132

      Use case 3: Automated Ticket Resolution 133

      Introduction 133

         High-level Process 134

         Detailed Process 134

         High-level Solution 136

         Detailed internal view of the selected automation components 138

         Solution Realization of Use cases 139

   Conclusion 140

6. Enterprise Automation Journey 141

   Introduction 141

   Structure 142

   Objective 142

   Challenges in Enterprise Automation 142

      Absence of a defined strategy 144

      Siloed Automation across enterprise 145

      Unclear ROI 145

Resistance in Automation Adoption 146
Lack of an Operating Model 146
Complex technology architecture 147
Scarcity of suitable resources 147
Journey Towards Intelligent Automation 148
Automation Center of Excellence 150
Need for Automation Center of Excellence 151
Functions of Automation CoE 153
Organization 155
Different models of CoE 155
Centralized CoE Model 156
Federated CoE 157
Hybrid Model 157
Process 160
Technology 163
Governance 165
Setting Up a CoE 166
Conclusion 166
Further Reading 167

7. **Intelligent Automation – Trends and the Future** 169
Introduction 169
Structure 170
Objective 170
Process Mining 171
Importance of process mining in the context of
Intelligent Automation 173
List of Prominent Process Mining Tools 176
Citizen Development 177
Rising Trend of Citizen Development 177
Citizen Development Platforms in Intelligent Automation 179

Pitfalls of Citizen Development *181*
List of Tools *182*
AIOps 183
Working of AIOps *184*
AIOps Platforms *187*
Future of work 188
Dimensions of Future of Work *188*
Conclusion 191
References 192

Index **193-199**

CHAPTER 1
Introduction to Intelligent Automation

Introduction

Automation today is an important buzzword in most businesses across the various industries and domains. Today, the majority of C–suite executive discussions on strategy and enterprise roadmap have an element of automation in it. It has crossed that stage where the CxOs no longer enquire about *"Why"* automation is needed; they are more interested in *"How"* they can get started. The interest in automation has only increased in the times of the pandemic. Today, as the enterprises have a significant resource pool working from their homes, the automation in business and IT processes have become more significant than ever. Gartner had listed Hyper Automation as one of the top technology trends of 2020 and the trend has accelerated now.

In this chapter, we will discuss and understand this trend in the context of Automation in Information Technology, and how it has now become one of the important imperatives to transform the businesses across industries.

The automation journey is long and transformational, and we will understand the different stages of automation that exist within the enterprises before finally embarking on what Intelligent Automation in an enterprise means.

Being transformational, automation is likely to have a significant impact on the business and enterprise in terms of organization culture and nature of workforce. The concept of *"Future of work"* is evolving as I write and has a close relationship to the way Automation, and specifically, Intelligent Automation is going to evolve in the days to come.

Structure

In this chapter, we will cover the following topics:

- Evolution of Automation
- What are the different stages of Automation?
- Intelligent Automation with examples
- Components of Intelligent Automation
- Impact of Automation in an enterprise
- Future of work

Objective

After studying this chapter, you should be able to articulate clearly the concept of Intelligent Automation and describe in detail the technologies of Intelligent Automation. You should also be able to discuss the applicability of Intelligent Automation through examples and appreciate the concept of future of work.:

Introduction to Automation

By definition, automation is a technology by which a process can be performed with minimal human intervention.

Automation has been prevalent since ages. The invention of the wheel can probably be considered as the earliest example of automation which helped the early humans move things from one place to another. The simple machines that we learn about in school like lever, pulley, and wedges are also the extremely basic examples of automation.

Since then, technology has advanced in leaps and bounds – from steam engines to self-driven cars, mankind has been experiencing it all. The human race discovered the machines to make it easier to do the work and reach a desired outcome, and the concept behind this is automation.

The primary goal of automation is, thus, to take the load off from human resources for the repeatable and manual tasks. In information technology, the computer programs themselves are the pieces of automation. Since then, we have been practicing automation through scripts, macros, batch processes, the integration of different applications, and more recently, workflows, specialized programs like robotic process automation, and many others. These computer programs remove the burden of the repetitive tasks through automation, as well as boost productivity, reliability, and accuracy of the task.

In this book, our domain of discussion will be around the automation in IT systems, that is, the automation that can be achieved through the computer programmable components. We will discuss the *"what"*, *"why"* and *"how"* of the automating business and IT processes in an enterprise and the impacts of this automation in the overall business and IT ecosystem.

In this introductory chapter, we will talk about the different stages of automation leading to the matured state of Intelligent Automation, through the software components and computer programs – many of which are available and rendered as off-the-shelf software products, technology paradigms, and open-source libraries.

Process, people, and technology are the key pillars in an enterprise. Automation spans across these three pillars, which is why the impact of automation cuts across all these layers of an enterprise. Automation, across industries, has thus become one of the key drivers in the business operating models today.

Evolution of automation in Information Technology

Automation has been practiced in the context of Information Technology since long. One of the objectives of introducing computer systems itself was to do the computations automatically. If you have seen the movie *"Hidden Figures"*, the story revolves around how the NASA employed bright and intelligent people, mainly women, good in mathematics as their *"Computer"* resources; however, with the advent of automation with computers, NASA brought in the mainframes to accelerate the computing process and these *"Computer"* resources became the initial batch of programmers building automation.

This story illustrates an important perspective. Information technology was the force that brought automation into hitherto purely manual tasks of calculation, tabulation, aggregation, sorting, processing, and reporting. Between the 1950s and today, the IT automation narrative has evolved, in a sense, reaching the levels where we are automating even the supervisory controls that humans exercise, simply put – automating the automation itself.

Let us now look at how this evolution happened. But for that, we need to first understand the IT architectural constructs of those times that led to people figuring out ways to reduce the onerous activities.

1970s-80s

The business IT architectures of these times were typified by centralized processing, using the mainframe technology. As these mainframe technologies were expensive to own and operate, there were centralized **Electronic Data Processing (EDP)** units in the organizations that operated these machines. The mainframes typified the server centric, compute intensive batch processing jobs, that replaced significant manual activities. The user interfaces were *"dumb terminals"*, and line printers. This is the environment where we come across the first examples of automation in information technology.

In general, these departments were manned not by computer scientists, but by *"geeks"* that understood *"how"* computers worked. The very beginnings of automation in information technology can be seen in the shell scripts that the personnel in the EDP departments wrote. These shell scripts ran in the OS environment and orchestrated the flow of the distinct batch processing programs in succession, and were often controlled by the rudimentary decision logic built into the script.

1980s-90s

This is a very interesting period as it was at the cusp of a radical rethink in the Business-IT architecture. In my view, it was led by two great forces – one of which was *economic* and the other was the evolution of *technology*.

Economically speaking, more companies outgrew their traditional markets and struck up the operations overseas, often under disparate regulatory regimes, even as the multilateral trade agreements came into effect facilitating such expansions.

Technologically speaking, rapid advances in chip miniaturization meant that it was possible to produce more powerful and smaller computers than the mainframe behemoths. Taking advantage of these newer computers (midrange, as they were known) were the robust Unix operating systems complete with their third-generation programming languages and the beginnings of professional grade data management applications (Oracle and Sybase).

This is known as the age of client-server architecture – the servers were typically these Unix boxes and the clients ranged from the early dumb green screens to the later thick clients running on Windows 95/98, often with a presentation and/or a business logic.

So, when the compute got distributed to the siloed operations spread all over the globe, it became more important than ever, especially to the top management to use the *information* that their operations generated. So, the first use of Integration, as we know it, was really the beginnings of **Electronic Data Interchange** (**EDI**) – the earliest examples of which were the offices exchanging the text files of the business transactions over the telephone line.

So, why is this important to the story of automation? The answer lies in the need to reliably perform the Integration over the network – and during those days, this was done using point-to-point connections over the telephone (yes, the internet hadn't arrived till then).

As the telephone network was undeniably unreliable for the data in motion, for the first time, automation was used to verifiably exchange the complete data streams between the servers, often hundreds of miles apart.

90s-00s

This period saw a major transformation with the internet and the dot com boom. The highlight of this period was the internet-based communication that enabled communication and interoperability between different disparate systems. The three-tiered and n-tiered web-oriented architecture with thin client (browser) in the frontend, application server, and databases gave rise to the transformation of many business models. This was built on the automation of the previous architectural paradigms and was further refined.

This period also gave rise to automation in the IT development. With fast-paced acceleration in building websites, the automated code generation tools in the form of IDEs that created the initial skeleton for the development activities were in demand. The interoperability between the systems required common entity and data models and common integration models with defined interfaces, so that the business entities could flow between the different tiers spread across the distributed systems, resulting in automation of several consumer facing processes.

The automation in this era was also in the form of workflows that integrated the application and data across different systems, connected over the internet. The companies exposed their consumer facing workflows to the internet or intranet depending on the nature of the user base. The online travel reservations and the online retail (remember the first website of Amazon?) started gaining popularity.

00s-10s

This period marked the beginning of the Cloud era with a transformation in how the software applications and platforms were hosted. The cloud architecture further emphasized on the modular application architecture preferably hosted on the containers that can be lifted and shifted, and run on different cloud platforms as independent entities. The cloud era further accelerated the workflow process automation that went across the on-premise applications to the cloud hosted ones. This also gave rise to significant automation in the way the IT environments are provisioned and IT applications are developed, tested, and deployed. The DevOps automation, targeted at automating the code development, integration, test and deployment on the target platforms, started gaining momentum. This automation in DevOps increased the speed of development and deployment, increased accuracy and reliability, and automated the software release management process.

10s-20s

Through this evolution that we discussed earlier, we see that automation has existed in the information technology industry for quite a while. However, it picked up pace as a key imperative for the business in this decade when the whole IT industry was striving *"to do more with less"*. Few industries like banking and functional areas like finance and accounting led the way. With the paradigms like Digital Front Office and Digital Transformation, and technologies like **Robotic Process Automation (RPA)** and **AI (Artificial Intelligence),** automation evolved beyond academics and research and became commercially viable. Its integration and interoperability with microservices, availability of Cloud services at infrastructure, platform, and software application level, all added up to make the environment ripe for the business process automation.

The initial automation transformation was driven by scripts, macros, and workflows, and was later followed by RPA that targeted the automation of repetitive rules based processes in the enterprise. The back-office IT operations were a low hanging fruit for automation since it mostly involved moderately well-defined processes. The structured system data in the well-defined systems of record in most enterprises further made the automation of these processes feasible. Many early adopters went ahead and automated their back-office processes and reaped the business benefits. But these were mostly disjoint activities and tasks like access management, automatic ticket logging, alert notification, and so on. As the technologies matured, the enterprises started to identify the value of automating the business processes end to end, but lacked the defined strategy to drive this and the maturity to implement the same. Even today as I write, though ~60% of the enterprises in the US have some form of automation, it's less than 10% that have built an automation ecosystem at scale.

Coming back to the present day – today, automation exists in all facets of business – be it in banking to automotive or insurance to healthcare. The self-driven automatic cars, automatic payments, voice assisted online shopping – automation now encompasses all the functions and is becoming an integral part of our existence; *Siri* and *Alexa* are our children's play assistants as much as ours.

Traditionally, automation was considered as a lever to reduce the manual labor (thus cost), and increase the accuracy and reliability of the functions in most scenarios. However, in today's world, the benefits of automation are manifold – from the lower operating costs to quick and accurate operations, from reduced time to market to optimization of the business processes – these are just some of the significant ones.

Thus, automation is enabled in the scope of IT with software components like robotic process automation, virtual assistants and chatbots, workflows and integration, and many other technical components, which we will discuss in the later sections.

Based on what I have seen in my years of working in automation, enterprises are at different levels or stages of automation. This is based on whether the automation consists of individual tasks and activities, individual sub-processes and processes and end-to-end automation of multiple processes encompassing a user's journey. This also depends on the technological maturity of the technology leveraged for the implementation and scaling the automation beyond a few use cases across the enterprise.

In this following section, we will discuss in detail the different levels of automation that we typically find in an enterprise.

Different Stages of Automation

In today's world, automation is one of the key drivers in the enterprise. But the enterprises are at different levels in its adoption of automation. Some industries like banking and automotive are some of the early adopters and somewhat ahead of the curve in the automation adoption.

The ultimate vision, with respect to automation, is to transform to a state where people augment their capability of doing work, leveraging the power of automation. This automation is provided by the different technological components which make up the digital workforce like chat bots, RPA bots, workflows, integration, and many other technological components. When we say digital workforce, they are enabled by the combination of various technological components that serve as the levers of automating a process, activity, or task.

In an enterprise with matured level of automation, most activities or processes that can be automated is automated partially or wholly. Artificial intelligence drives the decision of what action needs to be executed and the execution of the action is done by digital workforce.

However, in many enterprises which may be less matured in terms of automation, there may be only a small percentage of processes which are automated or semi-automated, and a large part of the activities and tasks are still required to be performed by humans. As mentioned before, we have observed through working experiences with large and small enterprises that there are some distinct stages of automation, based on how it has been implemented, what kind of data it operates on, what benefits it has delivered, and how it has been adopted by the enterprises at scale.

These different stages can be defined as follows:

- Basic automation
- Intermediate automation
- Intelligent automation

Take a look at the following diagram for a clear view of the stages of automation:

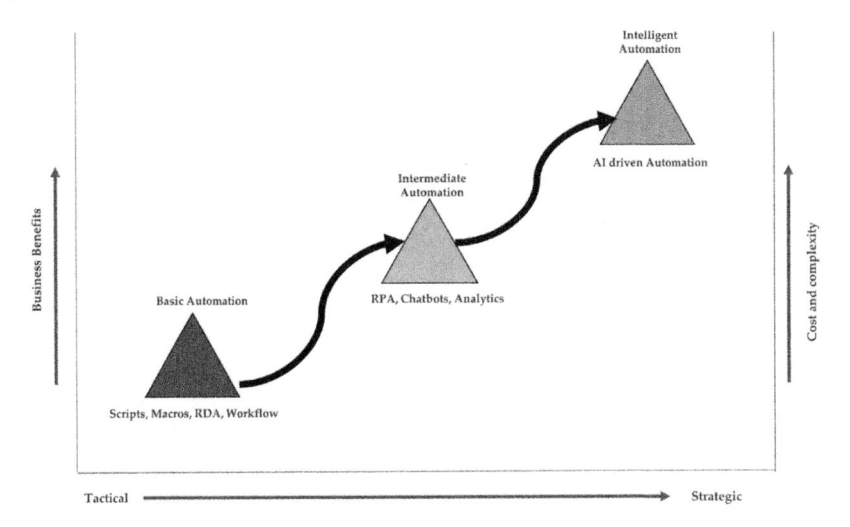

Figure 1.1: Stages of Automation

Basic automation

Basic automation exists in most enterprises in some form or the other. This type of automation includes different macros, scripts, batch processes etc. that exist mostly in the IT systems. For example, automated mail notification. In this type of use case, when an error has occurred, or when the mail file size becomes high, or a daily batch process is initiated, an automated notification is triggered at a certain frequency each time the event occurs. It could be a mail notification or some other defined action that needs to be executed. This is a very basic form of automation.

Basic automation usually involves the IT systems and point solutions around a specific task. They usually automate a definite set of tasks and activities. There is no inherent intelligence to the automation, and it is limited to the execution of certain transactions which are triggered externally.

In this type of automation, the process aspect of the automation is not given much importance; it's centered around a defined set of repetitive and labor-intensive tasks that need to be automated – in many cases, we see mostly the swivel chair type of automation. The tasks that are automated are also based on a definite set of business rules which can be easily programmed and executed. This automation is mostly for a single role of user. It may not be specifically tied to any technology and can be created and configured through most packaged and custom IT solutions.

An advanced form of basic automation is robotic desktop automation. In this type, specific repeatable tasks pertaining to a user is automated through a specific set of software solutions. In this type of automation, the software bot, which is a programmable component, mimics the actions of a human and executes the exact steps/tasks/activities that a human worker would execute. This type of automation needs human intervention and monitoring. The robotic desktop automation software is typically installed on the user's machine, and can perform screen scraping, file transfers, spreadsheet manipulations, report generation, and other simple transactions for the user. With robotic desktop automation, the process flavors are gradually brought into basic automation. A simple process which does not need manual intervention and is rule based can be automated through RDA. This automation must be triggered and driven by a human agent. From a scalability perspective, we need to keep in mind that this automation is installed on a user's machine, is not deployed on a server, and can be used for processes which are comparatively simple.

Intermediate automation

Intermediate automation builds on the foundations set up by the basic automation. In this stage, we move from the task-based automation to a process-focused automation. The robotic process automation is a key driver in this stage. RPA, which will be described in detail in the next chapter, can mimic the human behavior like comparing the data across screens, reading the data displayed on the screens, matching the data between the applications, and similar actions. With intermediate automation, more complex processes are taken up for automation, in which there can be planned handoffs to the human agents or other systems. This is usually achieved through an orchestration between the participating systems or participating automation levers to choreograph the process. To complement this, in the intermediate automation stage, there are enterprises which start building the foundation for the AI systems. There can be virtual assistants, which can communicate and chat with the users (business or consumer), understand the context and issue of the communication, and execute the relevant transaction through an RPA bot, or an API, or a microservice, or any other transaction processing system prevalent in the enterprise. However, in this stage, the AI is still not matured and is still evolving. The goal in this stage is to achieve an end-to-end automation in a scalable ecosystem for the tasks that are repeatable, labor intensive, primarily rules based, and mostly works on the structured data.

In the intermediate automation, the RPA bots are the drivers of the automation. The associated AI and the other technological components are in a supporting mode, aiding the RPA bots with the decisions/recommendations as required. The focus in this stage is primarily to increase the efficiency, reduce manual effort, and gain productivity.

To explain with an example, let us describe a scenario. An IT ecosystem has many systems, application management, and monitoring tools. There is usually a separate team of people who manage and monitor these systems for alerts and errors. Imagine a type of automated system, where as soon as the error occurs, there is an automation component that intercepts this error and triggers the right resolution action. The action could be executed by a bot, a microservice, an API call, and so on. The result is a system that can auto resolve a **known** error as it arises. This could be an example of the intermediate automation stage in an enterprise.

What is important to keep in mind is that in this stage, the underlying data is still primarily structured data, but there could be pockets of unstructured data that need focus, so that they slowly start building the foundation for the next stage of automation. For example, in the virtual assistant example, where the chatbot is communicating with the end user, there will be unstructured data that the chatbot needs to be trained on, to interpret the conversation. In addition to this, there will be significant structured data to determine what action is to be taken based on the event identified by the chatbot. To summarize, in this stage, the RPA tends to mimic the human actions and drives the automation and AI or Artificial Intelligence (which will be detailed out in *Chapter 3, Artificial Intelligence*) is in a supplemental mode and meant for augmenting the human ability.

Intelligent Automation

The third stage is what we call Intelligent Automation; it is the main topic of this book. This is a stage where the processes in an enterprise are automated, adaptive and are intelligent. This means that the processes can execute without manual intervention, or with minimal human intervention. Most human actions can be mimicked, and the system can sense and react to the different external and internal triggers. This stage is also built on the foundations laid down by the first and second stages.

With AI becoming one of the key driving technologies today, there is a strong motivation to combine AI with the traditional RPA based automation to achieve this stage. As AI is infused into the processes, they acquire the ability to intercept, understand, and react to the different business and IT events in the ecosystem. With AI, self-learning and reasoning can also be infused which makes the process intelligent. The result is a process that can respond to the different events and triggers in the ecosystem with different actions to respond to the occurrence, just like the way in which a human would respond. For example, say in the monitoring system, a set of alerts are recurring. In a traditional situation, what would we have done? Get an SME to analyze the logs and identify if any action needs to be taken to proactively prevent any failure. In case of an intelligent system, exactly on similar lines, the system can predict, based on this occurrence, whether there is a probability of a critical system to go down and become unavailable. If the probability of that occurrence crosses a certain threshold, the intelligent system will trigger a set of actions to resolve and remediate the downtime causing error. This is a very simple example of Intelligent Automation.

In intelligent automation, automation of the selected process is enabled end-to-end using multiple technology levers based on their fitment to achieve the best result. There could be the natural language processing, predictive modeling, and the others along with the orchestrated bots that complete the automation of the process. What is important to remember is how the convergence of technologies to achieve the automation is benefitting the business.

To define Intelligent Automation, it is the type of automation where multiple exponential technologies like *AI, Blockchain, IoT, Robotic Process Automation, Workflows,* and *Integration* are brought in together to automate a process end-to-end and infuse intelligence into it, so that it can react suitably and learn from the reactions. This is the essence of Intelligent Automation.

As opposed to the intermediate stage, in Intelligent Automation, the AI systems primarily drive the automation. Within the process being automated, it identifies/predicts/recommends the action that needs to be executed. The intelligence of the Intelligent Automation system decides *'what is to be done'*, and an RPA bot or the other technological components like microservices, etc. execute that action.

We need to keep in mind, the transformation to Intelligent Automation therefore calls for a major shift in the data management approach for the enterprise, among the other things. We are now dealing with a multitude of data sources and data types to derive the recommendations and insights, and that calls for a strategic approach to the information architecture. As they say, there can be no AI without **Information Architecture (IA)**.

If we go back to the alert automation example of the intermediate automation, let us now understand how the same process transforms in Intelligent Automation.

There can be different flavors to that alert management process. Let us consider the scenario where before any alert arises, there are warnings and other messages on the logs across the different systems. In intelligent automation, the intelligent components can derive the insights from these messages and predict events. For example, by the analysis of certain log messages and warnings across systems, it can predict that an alert will occur, and based on that prediction, there may be a bot which can execute the resolution action.

As the automation in the enterprise matures from the basic to intermediate to intelligent, the focus of the automation shifts from task-based to process-based to process + data based. In basic automation, the primary goal of automation is to 'do' the action. As it moves to Intelligent Automation, the primary goal shifts to 'think', 'do', and 'learn'. This is a major shift in how we design, build, configure, and deploy our systems. To reiterate, the journey to Intelligent Automation needs to be a well thought out strategy, and should be planned and executed accordingly, keeping in mind, the scale and return on investment for an enterprise.

Automation of tasks, activity, and processes

When we are talking about automation in an enterprise, it is very important to understand the context and level of abstraction that we are talking about. Typically, when we discuss automation, its benefits, and the ROI, we talk with reference to the processes. What this means is, instead of talking of automation at tasks or activity level, for meaningful business conversation, it makes sense to quantify automation at the level of processes and functional process areas.

The processes are the core to any business. A process is a set of tasks and activities which are performed by certain roles in an enterprise in a predefined way to achieve a definite outcome. This outcome could be related to a business or revenue goal, business KPI, or the other metric in the enterprise. For example, opening a new account would be a business process in the context of banking, provisioning a mobile number would be a business process in Telecom, logging a service request would be a process in IT operations, and so on.

Typically, in an enterprise, there are different process blocks – like front office processes, mid office processes, and back office processes. Each process block has many process areas – like the back office can have HR, IT Services etc., the front office can have Customer Relations, Contact Center etc., and the mid office can have Lending in case of banks. These make up the primary building blocks in an enterprise. In this book, we will keep referring to the processes and process areas in the context of automation, and hence it is important to understand this now. The following diagram will give a better idea about this structure:

Introduction to Intelligent Automation | 15

Front Office
- Digital Channels
- Customer Acquisition
- Contact Center
- Other process areas..
- Other process areas..

Middle Office
- Order Management
- Account Management
- Billing
- Other process areas..
- Other process areas..

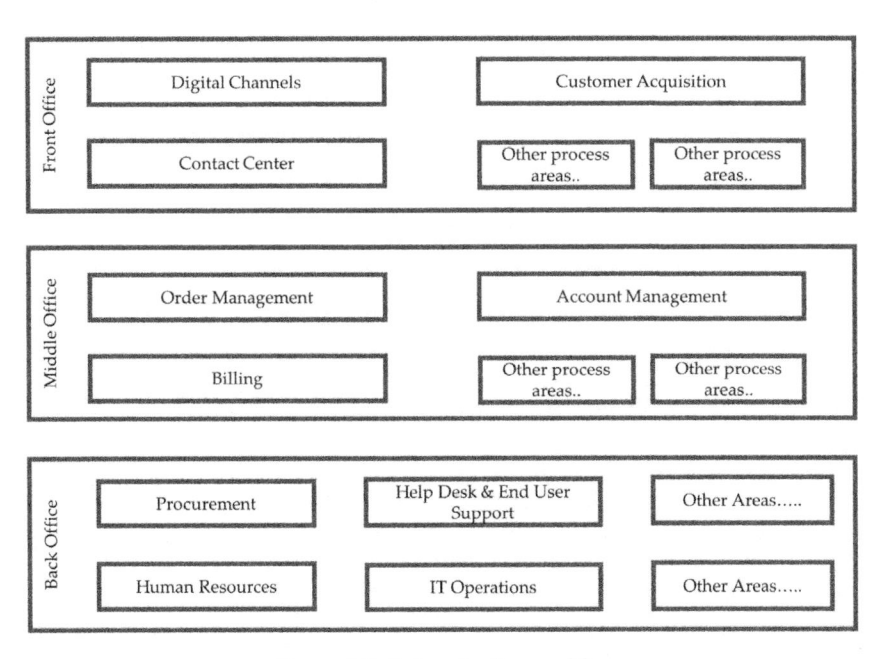

Back Office
- Procurement
- Help Desk & End User Support
- Other Areas.....
- Human Resources
- IT Operations
- Other Areas.....

Figure 1.2: *Enterprise Process Map*

As you can see in the preceding diagram, within each of the block, like the front office or the middle office, there are process areas like Account Management, Lending etc. in Banking, Order to Cash in Retail, and so on. These process areas will have multiple processes which are further decomposed into sub processes, activities, and tasks.

Understanding this structure about the processes is very important in automation. These process, sub process, activities, and tasks are all candidates for automation at different levels. We could start with automating a critical task as a proof on concept and then extend it to cover the activity and process. Hence, the adequate analysis of processes and its constituents and identifying the levers at each level is very essential for the successful automation.

Traditionally, we have seen that the processes in any enterprise are enabled, operated, and supported by the people in the enterprise. The procurement specialists supporting the procurement processes or the customer service agents handling the Contact Center queries are good examples of the people supporting the processes. There are usually the IT operation teams who manage and execute the IT processes.

To execute these different processes, the people are enabled by different technological solutions – it could be an Enterprise Resource Planning System or a Customer Relationship Management System or a Ticket Management solution, or many others that are relevant to the processes.

With automation, there is a shift in this symbiotic relationship between the process, the people, and the technology. With automation emerging as a key driver for many C-Suite Executives, the way they plan to operate and execute the processes is changing. Enabled by automation, the processes will be run by the technology – which may be composed of bots, virtual assistants, and other digital workforce components. The technology will be supported by the human workforce. In case the technology is unable to execute the action, human support will be sought for. Many enterprises today are planning and actively driving the *"No Touch Operations"* as one of their key imperatives.

However, this does not mean in any way that the human workers will be redundant – they will not be. They will be reskilled and upskilled to perform those tasks that cannot be performed by a machine – bots, virtual assistants, and the other elements of digital workforce. The future of work will see a close coordination and coexistence of such a hybrid workforce. We will discuss the Future of Work in a later section.

Examples of Intelligent Automation

Now that we have understood the different stages of automation and the journey to reach Intelligent Automation, let us try to explore some examples of Intelligent Automation. The following are mostly generic examples across the different processes prevalent in the industry:

- **Automated Email processing**: In this type of use case, the intelligent system will automatically read the email text and understand the key message being conveyed. Based on that, it will recommend the follow up actions which will be orchestrated and triggered by a bot/microservices/downstream API etc. The email can have a fixed structure with key elements of information that needs to be filled in, defined or an unstructured, free form text email.

- **Automated Invoice processing**: This is one of the most common use cases that is usually selected as a prime candidate for automation. In this scenario, the invoices are generated from the suppliers and sent for payment. In the process, the invoices need to be validated and matched, the key data elements need to be copied into the accounting system, and finally approved for payment. In a pure RPA implementation (somewhere in the Intermediate Automation stage), the RPA bot would download the invoices, save in a specific location, open the invoices. and copy-paste the information (assuming the invoices have a specific format) to the accounting system. In case of the ambiguous invoices or incorrect formats, the bot would be unable to process and hand over to a human agent for assistance. As the enterprise moves from intermediate to Intelligent Automation, this implementation also gets refined.

Take a look at the following diagram to get a better understanding of the invoice processing generic process:

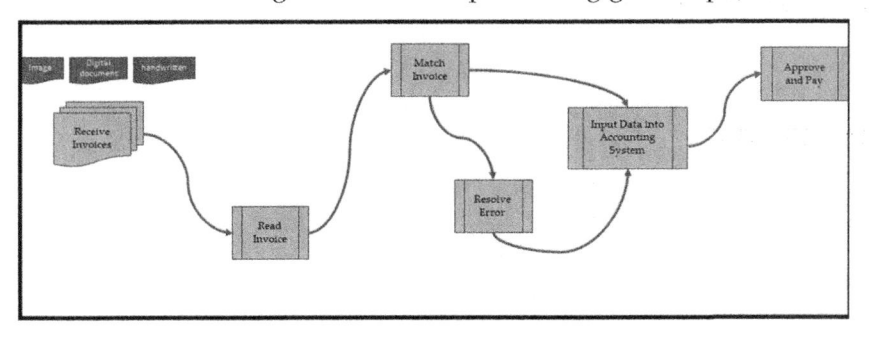

Figure 1.3: Invoice Processing Generic Process

- The processing of purchase orders by digitally capturing the purchase orders, retrieving the key information from the purchase orders and routing the purchase orders to the relevant stakeholders and storing them in the enterprise system of record – this is a familiar example of invoice processing with similar challenges around the interpretation of correct data.
- Another example of Intelligent Automation which are becoming very common these days are virtual assistants. These chatbots enabled by AI can converse in a natural language and disseminate the various types of *"how to"*

- information. In an advanced version, these chatbots can help the user execute the different transactions as well.

- Intelligent automation would also be beneficial in those processes where there are a lot of documents like paper invoices, to be read and interpreted, decisions to be made based on the data in the documents, and appropriate actions to be triggered.

These are just a few examples, and the opportunity of intelligent automation in an enterprise is enormous. There are many other examples of the processes that are fit for Intelligent Automation across the industries where AI and many other technologies work together to orchestrate the intelligently automated processes. In the following section, we will dive into the technologies that work together to make the Intelligent Automation real.

Intelligent automation technology components

In this section, let us explore the technological constituents on Intelligent Automation.

Intelligent Automation, as the name suggests, is the combination of intelligence with the automation technologies. Based on the understanding of the different levels of automation in the previous section, we can say that Intelligent Automation will include the Robotic Process Automation and Artificial Intelligence. But that is not all. When we talk about Intelligent Automation, it is basically the convergence of several technologies coming together and working in tandem. The primary technologies that are essential for Intelligent Automation can be listed as follows:

- Robotic Process Automation
- Artificial Intelligence
- Business Intelligence and Analytics
- Workflows and Business Process Management
- Integrations and Orchestrations
- Blockchain, Internet of Things (IoT)

- Chatbots (adding them separately from AI, since these are becoming de facto, specifically in the end user facing process automation)

Let us take a look at the following diagram for an understanding of the various automation technologies:

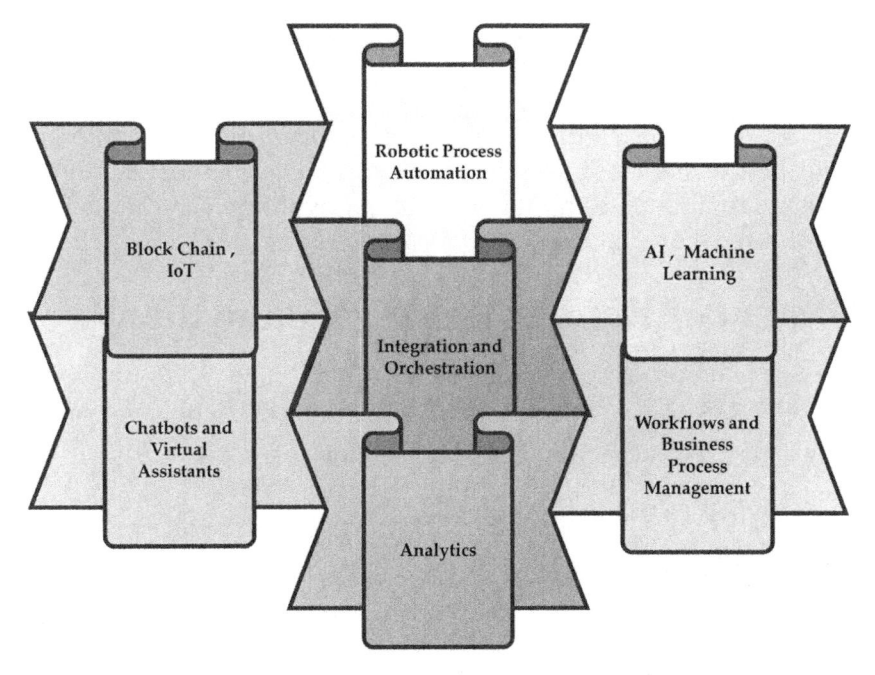

Figure 1.4: Intelligent Automation Technologies

Each of these pillars has sub-components or capabilities which are applicable in Intelligent Automation. In this section, we will discuss these technologies at a higher level to give you a sense of how they work together. In the following chapters, we will dive deep into each of these technologies one by one, where we will understand the fitment of these technologies with the relevant use cases in the context of Intelligent Automation.

Robotic Process Automation

Robotic Process Automation, as the name suggests, is one of the key technology components of Intelligent Automation. With RPA, we can create software components which, by acting like a bot, can automate processes. RPA can mimic the execution of human tasks and actions like data entry and modification, comparison of data, copying data across applications, creating reports, sending notifications, and so on. Since it mimics the human-computer interactions, RPA works on the business applications just like a human would do.

In the robotic process automation, we program and create the software *'robots'* to handle the repetitive, rule-based tasks, so that the human intervention can be reduced. In RPA, the interactions of the user with the different application user interfaces can be mimicked and hence automated.

Automating the repetitive tasks in an enterprise saves significant time, hence money, and improves accuracy. The robotic process automation, thus frees up the human bandwidth which can then be used for the more value-added tasks.

Fitment of Robotic Process Automation

The key characteristics of process, activity, and task for being automated by the Robotic Process Automation are as follows:

- Based on deterministic business rules.
- Repetitive in nature.
- Works on structured data.
- Executed in a digitized environment (i.e., does not include manual transfer of paper, files etc.).

We will discuss each of these factors in detail in *Chapter 2, Robotic Process Automation*.

A few examples of RPA can be listed as follows:

- Creation of tickets based on structured and templatized user emails.
- Health checks of applications or databases.
- Copying Data between applications; for example, in health insurance, we might need to look for certain data in the hospital systems and copy that data back into the insurance payer's system.

Depending on the nature of the use case, the different tools may have different levels of fitment to the use case requirements. As mentioned earlier, we will touch upon each technology, the relevant tools and frameworks, and the preferred practices in the subsequent chapters.

What is important to understand is where can we apply RPA in a large enterprise, and how to drive to that decision. The use cases or processes to be automated should determine the RPA product selection (or any other technology selection) and not the other way around.

It is also very important to understand that in an enterprise, we do not implement a technology solution just for the sake of it or just to be ahead of the technology curve. We do technology implementations to solve business problems and generate business benefits. The alignment of technology with business is of supreme importance to get the returns of investment on any technology. So, in this case as well, it is important to understand which of these are valid use cases that can generate the required ROI.

Additionally, if the use case is so complex that the cost of development of RPA far supersedes the benefit generated, then there is very little business value to get out of it. In this context, the labor intensity of the process to be automated is usually one of the more important considerations that impact the potential savings.

Benefit realization is an important topic in the overall automation transformation journey for an enterprise, and how to realize the benefits is a common concern. We have talked to many leaders of enterprises, and they have explained how even after a complex RPA development and deployment journey, the business benefits were not met. There may be many reasons for that to happen – external and internal factors. And this is not only the case with RPA; this can happen with any of the technology solutions. In the later chapters on how to scale automation, we will discuss how to ensure that we have a valid business case before getting into the design and development of automation.

Artificial Intelligence (AI)

Artificial Intelligence is a very broad topic. It refers to the technology in which we can infuse the elements of human intelligence like sensing, reasoning, interpretation, understanding, analysis etc. into the machines. In the context of this book, we will use AI as the technology that can infuse and embed intelligence in the software programs for the purpose of automation. From an Intelligent Automation perspective, this convergence with AI is what makes the automation intelligent. As explained in the previous sections, in the context of Intelligent Automation, AI is the brain of the system which determines how the system should react, and what actions should be executed, and RPA could be the limbs of the system that will actually execute the action.

In our context, we will be interested in the application of AI around the following:

- Natural language processing
- Image recognition
- Reasoning
- Self-learning and inferencing
- Speech recognition
- Sentiment analysis
- Text analysis

With these capabilities infused into the system, the decisions and actions can be derived automatically which otherwise would need human intervention.

In this context, there is another term which is used interchangeably with AI – that is, Machine Learning. You must have seen people talking about the AI/ML solutions. Machine Learning is a subset of AI. In machine learning, we use algorithms and statistical models on a set of data to identify the patterns and arrive at decisions and predictions without being explicitly programmed for them. Like the way in which we humans learn with experience, machine learning enables the system to learn and improve with usage based on the training that we conduct on the system. Machine learning enables the computer programs to learn without being explicitly programmed for it. Typically, the machine learning models can be used to identify the relationships and trends in data that might otherwise not be apparent. Machine Learning, Deep learning, image analysis, and sentiment analysis are available today as services from most of the leading players in the field of AI.

Let us now explore a few use cases in AI that are relevant when discussing Intelligent Automation.

A chatbot, which is an AI application with natural language processing, can understand the intent of the conversation. In a real implementation, the chatbot will converse with the user, can understand and disambiguate if necessary, and even use that information to arrive at an action. This action can be executed by RPA or any other downstream systems. This is a very simple use case.

In more complex cases, AI may have to analyze the video footage and identify specific objects, and based on the result, execute the actions. For example, in a traffic scenario, based on the video footage from the road intersections, an automated traffic management system can detect the license plate of the car that jumped the red light, retrieve the owner's details, and create a ticket for penalty.

Now, let us understand when we should use these technologies in Intelligent Automation.

Fitment of AI components for automation

The key characteristics of process, activity, task automated Robotic Process Automation are as follows:

- Non-deterministic business rules
- Repetitive in nature
- Decision is based on analysis of very high volume of data (structured and unstructured)

We will discuss each of these factors in detail in *Chapter 3, Artificial Intelligence*.

Most leading Product and Services companies in IT have some offering related to the AI services, products, and frameworks. We have platforms and services from Google, Microsoft, IBM etc., which offer AI services or platforms on Cloud and help to design, build, deploy, and host the AI models. There are open-source libraries which offer a host of APIs with which we can also build our AI components.

Similarly, just like in the RPA technology, in the context of Artificial Intelligence, it's not the individual technologies that should be of primary importance, however cutting edge they may be. At the end, it's the value that we are getting out of the Automation (be it RPA or AI or a combination of both) that is more important than the technological components being another lever to automate the process.

Workflows and Business Process Management

Business Process Management is a way of designing and modeling the various business processes and managing and executing them while involving people and technology. The workflows can be considered as a subset of Business Process Management, a component that enables Business Process Management. A workflow is basically a set of activities and tasks that need to be executed to complete a process or subprocess. A workflow may have a set of simple sequential tasks, or it could comprise of several parallel workflows to achieve a business goal. Workflows usually focus on the set of tasks and the people executing them in a process, whereas Business Process Management covers a larger domain where it focuses on the processes in an organization or a business unit as a whole and their efficiency. BPM would typically be made up of multiple workflows, decision engines, other tools, and human personnel, all working in tandem toward more efficiency and optimization.

The workflow automation is a sure way to increase the efficiency of a process and optimize it. The redundancies are eliminated and the digital tracking capability of the workflow makes it easier to manage and monitor.

Automating a workflow to achieve process automation, as we have seen, is a part of the basic to intermediate automation stage in the enterprise automation journey. It is extremely important to automate the critical workflows in the enterprise as this lays down the foundation for more advanced automation. The workflow automation could appear to be less complex than some of the other levers of automation, like AI, since the technology has matured over time. Also, through the workflows, there can be a provision to include human interventions wherever needed, like approvals from supervisors, error scenarios, and so on. In the overall journey of automation, once the basic workflow is implemented for a process, say with 50% of the tasks automated, it creates a very fertile ground to bring in the other levers of automation as the enterprise matures. The workflows are key in orchestrating the actions between humans, bots, and the other automation components in the Intelligent Automation ecosystem. Another thought that I just want to initiate here is that the workflows, when optimized and automated, lay down the foundation of smarter workflows which is one of the directions that the Intelligent Automation paradigm is moving towards in the IT industry.

Fitment of workflow for Automation

The key characteristics of process or activity to be automated by a workflow implementation are as follows:

- Repetitive in nature.
- Need of more accuracy and standardization in the sequence of processing.
- Made of up a series of tasks dependent on each other involving difference user roles.

There can be numerous examples of workflow around us. In a bank, as we enter to open an account, there is an Account Opening workflow. In a hospital, there can be Patient Admission workflow. In IT systems, there can User Access workflow, leave application workflow, Onboarding new employee workflow, and so on. So, most business operations in even moderately mature organizations are made up of partially or wholly automated workflows. There are a lot of workflow automation software prevalent in the industry. In addition to the off-the-shelf products, most enterprises have custom workflows implemented in their ecosystems as well.

Conceptually, as you might have realized by now, workflow automation to some extent is like the Robotic Process Automation. However, RPA is traditionally better for discrete tasks and a workflow is usually better in cases where there are many tasks which are dependent on each other and need communication amongst the systems and human resources for completion. Hence, we can have an Invoice Management workflow, where some of the discrete tasks of matching the data across systems and copying the data to the accounting system can be done by RPA. The ambiguous data from invoices can be interpreted and resolved by AI, but the overall orchestration and communication/approval between departmental resources could be managed by the workflow.

Business Intelligence

Business Intelligence and Analytics use the enterprise data to provide insights and arrive at decisions. Business Intelligence and Analytics meaningfully convert the data into information that can be applied in the business ecosystem. A pertinent question that can come up here is how Business Intelligence and Analytics is then different from AI, because AI also helps us uncover the information from data. Very simply put, AI refers to human like intelligence. In the AI systems, the computer programs are designed and trained to act and react somewhat like how we humans do, BI has got more to do with using the data to display visualizations and uncover patterns.

Business Intelligence involves the collection, consolidation, and analysis of large volume of data to derive insights to help in decision making. This means, BI aids in decision making using the data analysis; however, it does not make decisions based on any rationale. BI takes the noise out of the data and tries to provide a clear picture but is not designed to provide a clear direction about how to use the information to arrive at a decision.

However, without getting further into the debate of AI vs BI, the key message we want to point out is that BI with its capability of analyzing the data does form an important pillar in the whole enterprise automation ecosystem. Another important area in this overlapping space is predictive analytics. This also happens to be an important component in the Intelligent Automation space. In predictive analytics based on the collection, collation, and analysis of data, certain outcomes can be predicted. For example, most online retailers use some form of predictive analytics to forecast what would be your next purchase based on certain items you recently bought, and based on that, they usually send out ads, promotions, and so on.

In an Intelligent Automation, say in an IT operations scenario, there can be a predictive model recommending that a specific system might go down in the next few hours based on the analysis of the logs, alerts, warning etc. in the IT ecosystem. The event is predicted by the predictive analytics component and a downstream action can be executed by a bot, for example, to reboot the specific hardware.

Fraud prevention and recommendation engines are a few good examples where predictive analytics is used very successfully.

Integration

Integration is another key component of enterprise automation. System Integration indicates the linking of different systems and applications in the ecosystem. As readers of this book with the experience that we have in the IT field, we all understand the importance of integration between the IT systems. For all the preceding components of Intelligent Automation that we talked about, they all leverage integration between the systems at some level or the other. In the context of automation, this is again one of the foundational components. If you think of processes – processes are enabled by different IT systems. For example, an Order to Cash process in Telecom is enabled by different applications like CRM, Billing, Provisioning etc. Without an integration between these systems, there cannot be any automation – there cannot be seamless processing which starts with the order entry in the CRM system, provisioning the order in the Provisioning systems, and finally billing in the Billing system. The order that is entered in the CRM changes its state at the different stages of the order life cycle and is enriched at each state. This is possible because of the interoperability between the systems and efficient integration. Without Integration, the scenario would be three discrete applications – CRM, Provisioning, and Billing – all storing some duplicate information and without any holistic view of the most important entity, the customer and the order.

Now, there is another term that is used very commonly and interchangeably with Integration, that is Orchestration. The way we understand, the difference between integrations and orchestration is that orchestration is integration in a specific context. The context can be a business process, a customer journey etc. Orchestration, therefore, portrays more value than pure vanilla integration in a business context.

The enterprise application integration is a very matured area and has numerous frameworks, patterns, tools, and topologies that are used for implementing the application integrations. For the readers of this book, this is a familiar area, and we will not cover Integration as a topic in detail but delve into it in the context of orchestrating the different automation components.

Virtual Assistants and Chatbots

We have put Virtual Assistants and Chatbots separately from AI. This is because. as we speak, chatbots and virtual assistants have become one of the integral components of Intelligent automation.

Think of a use case where a procurement specialist must modify Purchase Orders on the go without an access to the ERP system.

Such automated modifications can be enabled by a chat bot which can converse in natural language with the Procurement Specialist (business user), capture the relevant data, i.e., PO No, type, line item etc., what needs modification, and then pass on the data to a downstream lever – RPA bot or microservice – to modify the PO in the ERP system.

These are simple to moderately complex use cases depending on the nature of intents that need to be interpreted by the chatbot. However, these types of user-facing use cases go a long way in achieving customer satisfaction and providing excellence in customer and employee experience.

There are a multitude of service providers providing chat bots, chat bot frameworks, and open-source libraries to create such chatbots and virtual assistants. What is important is the nature of intents that the process should handle, the ease of configuring the intents and training the system, and finally the capability of orchestration of the process between chatbots, RPA bots, microservices and other technology components.

Blockchain and IoT

When we are automating the processes across the enterprise – both internal and external – security and data integrity are some of the important factors that come into play. This is where the blockchain technology comes into play. Since the blockchain can be distributed across multiple system and is immutable, it provides a certain level of transparency and auditability in the transactions. In fact, embedding the blockchain technology into the workflows to automate the transactions, adds security and eliminates the risk of fraud. Being a distributed ledger technology, the blockchain can go beyond the financial use cases to any transaction between the different parties that demand immutability of the ledgers. A convergence of AI, blockchain, workflows, and RPA would mean that any transaction between the parties could be completely automated with all the relevant control and compliance in place. And this convergence, as we discussed, is what Intelligent Automation is all about – convergence of exponential technologies to achieve end-to-end automation with minimum or no human intervention. However, this area is still emerging and, in the days to come, we will see greater leverage of the blockchain technology in the automating processes across the enterprise.

The IoT or the internet of things is another area that might have significant impact on automation. Though it's still emerging, there are significant promises for this technology to evolve. With the advent of 5G globally, there is a huge scope of the IoT becoming an integral part of Intelligent Automation.

Impact of Automation in an Enterprise

Intelligent Automation has emerged as one of the key business drivers today. Most CxO level strategy discussions have automation as an important topic nowadays.

Each of the constituent technologies of Intelligent automation as discussed earlier, offer significant business benefits. When an enterprise harnesses the power of all of these in the form of an Intelligent Automation journey, the possibilities are endless. They will be able to reduce cost, increase efficiency, deploy manpower to more value-added activities, increase productivity, and thus create a memorable customer and employee experience. Some of the organization level impacts are discussed as follows:

- Intelligent Automation is now an enterprise scale opportunity. With a vision to have automation powered and driven by AI, there needs to be a defined automation strategy that will guide the enterprise across the automation transformation journey. This should include strategies around how to detect opportunities early in the game. There needs to be a balance between the low hanging fruits and the strategic plays when it comes to the automation opportunities in the enterprise.

- Intelligent Automation can change the enterprise business – IT ecosystem in a significant manner. The business processes are the core to any enterprise and traditionally, the business processes are run by people. With Intelligent automation in place, the resource work pool dynamics changes – it slowly transforms into a hybrid workforce with humans and bots complementing each other.So the way we work changes as Intelligent Automation is brought in.

- Automation can provide cost savings and improvement in productivity and efficiency. It can reduce the time to market for new products and services, reduce the cycle time for various business operations, improve employee and customer experience, and provide the flexibility to deploy experienced human resources where they are more needed.

- As mentioned in the previous discussions, the business processes are core to the enterprise. Embarking on the automation journey, therefore, calls for a closer look at the processes as well. A redundant or inefficient process cannot magically change into an efficient automated process. The process re-engineering and optimization exercise should be understood and undertaken, if there is a need.

- Last, but not the least, is the organizational change. Intelligent automation will result in a change in skills of the personnel, policies in the organization, operations, and governance. Basically, it will have an impact on the way things are done currently in all the aspects of the enterprise. There needs to be a strong organizational change management in place when the automation transformation is happening. This will not only help in increased adoption of automation, but also have an impact on the personnel morale

Future of Work

Intelligent Automation has emerged as a significant driver, as well as a disruptor and has started to impact the way work will be done in the future.

As more and more processes and activities get automated partially or wholly, the rising concern of the people losing jobs will rise. Yes, as more and more repeatable jobs get automated, the people doing those activities will become redundant. However, there are several counter arguments in this regard. As automation increases, the skilled workforce needed to build and manage this automation will be on the rise. Also, the reengineered automated processes will give rise to new job requirements. What this means is, there is a clear indication of a shift in the skills for the future.

Secondly, automating repetitive, rule-based jobs is way less complex and inexpensive than automating the "thinking" jobs. Hence, the thinking skills will continue to be more valuable. The machines still do not have the communications skills and the emotional skills that we humans possess. The jobs requiring such skills like negotiations and interactions will still need the human touch to be productive and efficient.

As the automation journey continues, the machines and IT systems will become more and more intelligent. The need of the hour for the human workforce to get ready for the future of work is to become more adaptive. As the needs of the ecosystem evolve, we, the human workforce, need to evolve too. A balanced hybrid workforce is what most enterprises will strive to manage and maintain going forward, and the trend has already started. The human workforce needs to continuously unlearn and learn new ways of doing work, with new members in the organization – all of them may not be of the same breed as them. The humans in this hybrid workforce needs to be more and more engaged and empowered to keep the soul of the organization alight.

A well-known analyst firm mentioned a term Robotics Quotient – which is a measure of how well humans and machines will work together in the future. This might become a key metric along with emotional quotient (EQ), as we build the future workforce.

Intelligent Automation will impact the way businesses operate, manage resources, adopt culture, and serve clients. However, the core purpose of the organization will remain the same, i.e., to serve their clients in the relevant domain and provide the services to their customer. Hence, it becomes extremely important for the leaders of the organization to plan, execute, and manage this change and drive the enterprise towards a future with Intelligent Automation.

So, as we speak of the Future of Work, we should continue to learn and adopt new ways of doing work, improve our ability to adapt to new environments, build the skills like ideation, innovation, empathy, and communication which are our real differentiators, and focus on building a workplace with perfect synergy between the men and the machines.

Conclusion

By now, you must have got a good idea about the concept of Intelligent Automation, and what the different technologies that work together to create Intelligent Automation in an enterprise are. You should also have a fair idea about some of the use cases that we discussed briefly in this chapter, and why they can be categorized as the Intelligent Automation use cases.

To summarize, Intelligent Automation is that state of automation in which the system can execute the automated processes, can sense, reason, and interpret events, and execute actions accordingly with minimal or no human interactions. In today's world, it is one of the key imperatives of CxOs across all industries and domains.

Intelligent Automation represents the convergence of multiple exponential technologies which work in an orchestrated manner to achieve end-to-end automation. In this state, AI, RPA, Workflows, Integration, and many other technological elements work in tandem to enable end-to-end process automation.

The automation journey of an enterprise can be a multiyear, multi-dimensional journey –traversing through the different stages like basic and intermediate, and finally reaching the Intelligent Automation end state where it keeps on refining and optimizing its decisions and executions.

In the automation journey, it is very important to understand and formulate a strategy around benefit realization and Return on Investment. The processes that are selected for automation should be analyzed carefully from different dimensions to reap the maximum benefit from Intelligent Automation.

In the end, it will be good to emphasize on the fact that Intelligent Automation will have significant impact on how businesses are run. It will result in changes and shifts across the organization with respect to skills, policies, governance, and of course, the nature of workforce. All around the world, we are in the process of defining the *"Future of work"* which entails a synergy between the men and the bots with a hybrid workforce being prevalent across industries. We will touch upon that as we proceed through the next chapters.

Chapter 2
Robotic Process Automation

Introduction

The **World Economic Forum** (**WEF**) has come out with a report titled *"Will robots steal our jobs"* on "*robot revolution*", which says that automation will create 97 million jobs worldwide but will make almost the same number of jobs redundant. Some of the routine manual jobs like data processing, data entry, telemarketing, switchboard operators, bill and account collectors, and so on will very soon be replaced by the software bots. These bots are pieces of programmable software, coded to execute a set of activities. This disruption is being aggravated by the COVID-19 pandemic and is accelerating the pace of the adoption of automation across the world. What this indicates is that the Robotic Process Automation is becoming one of the key drivers in the automation landscape, and it is becoming imperative that its adoption will increase day by day.

With the business significance in mind, in this chapter on Robotic Process Automation, we will discuss and understand the Robotic Process Automation, its characteristics and benefits, and how to plan and start the RPA journey in an enterprise.

Structure

In this chapter, we will cover the following topics:
- Purpose of RPA
- Characteristics of RPA
- Benefits of RPA
- Best suited RPA use cases
- RPA best practices
- RPA products and tools

Objective

After reading this chapter, you should be able to understand the characteristics of Robotic Process Automation as a technology lever of automation and appreciate the benefits that is brought by implementing RPA in an enterprise. You should be able to determine which kind of processes are good fit for RPA based on a set of technical and business criteria through a few examples. Lastly you will know about the best practices about how to implement an RPA project and get an idea about some of the leading product vendors in this space.

Purpose of RPA

We have introduced that idea of Robotic Process Automation or RPA in *Chapter 1, Introduction to Intelligent Automation*. The primary purpose of RPA is to automate the tasks and activities that are repeatable, labor intensive, based on deterministic rules, works on structured digital data, and is executed in a digital system. It is usually used to automate those activities that are executed as a set of tasks in a sequence. Since it can mimic human activities, RPA can emulate the human interaction with different digital systems like opening a portal, data entry on application forms, data updates across screens, and the other swivel chair type activities. These types of activities usually follow the same steps over and over and are usually known and documented procedures. For example,, think of a person who is handling complaints and service requests and routing those to the relevant groups for resolution. An RPA bot that can mimic this activity, will be able to free up this resource and enable the person to engage in more essential activities. Hence, the goal is to free up the human labor and deploy them to more value-added tasks, increase efficiency, and reduce errors.

Characteristics of RPA

Robotic Process Automation is a way of automating business and IT processes through programmable software components called *'bots'*. The bots are programmed to perform a set of tasks and activities mimicking the activities of a human worker. They are usually programmed to perform repetitive, labor intensive tasks that follow a definite set of rules. Analysis or decision making is not a typical forte of RPA. But in recent times, there are different product companies that are offering *"Intelligent"* bots. We will discuss that towards the later part of this chapter. While mimicking human tasks, RPA also executes the tasks and activities faster and in an error-free mode. Since the bots don't make mistakes, don't sleep, and don't retire, they may be more efficient in doing certain type of jobs better than humans, thus, freeing up the human talent pool for more value-added work. Thus, the enterprises across the globe are seeing the benefits of RPA and are either already into their RPA journey or actively planning for it.

Key Characteristics

The robotic process automation, as a key lever of technology for Intelligent Automation, has a few distinct characteristics, as shown in the following diagram:

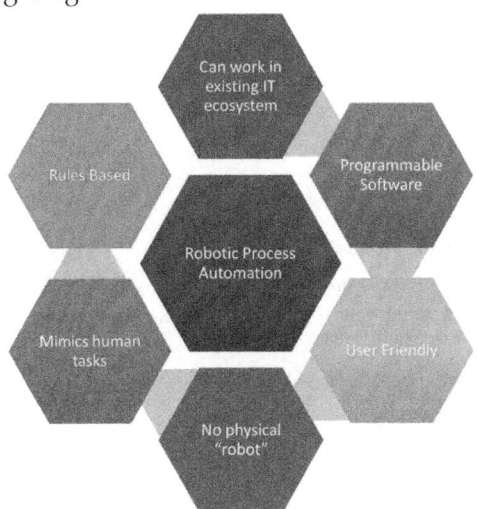

Figure 2.1: Characteristics of RPA

The main characteristics of RPA are listed as follows:

Programmable software:

RPA is a **programmable software** (and there is *no physical robot*), which is usually written in an integrated programming environment, typically provided by the product vendor. There are multiple companies that provide the RPA framework, platforms, and libraries with varying degrees of capability for process automation. Most of these products provide software development kits and an integrated development environment with drag and drop user interfaces that can be leveraged while creating new bots for an enterprise. Most RPA products and tools are pretty *user friendly* with Graphical User Interfaces (GUI) for the bot creator. As part of their execution, the RPA bots usually keep an audit trail which makes it easier to track and manage the activities of the virtual workforce.

Rule based

The RPA programs *imitate the exact actions* that the humans would perform. The interactions with the different applications through their UI, matching the data across the different applications, copying and pasting of a variety of information across multiple screens and applications, filling in and submitting the forms, sending emails etc., are typical use cases for the RPA implementation. For example, a simple bot can open an email, say with an invoice as an attachment, download the invoice attachment, and save the invoice in a predefined location in the file system. RPA can read the invoice if it's digital (no handwriting/images) and templatized (fixed data entity in fixed location in the form) and copy the data into the Accounting System. This is pretty much what an accounting clerk would do. The RPA bots do not need breaks, holidays, or vacations, and thus, they bring in more value for these repetitive, rule based, manual activities. In this context, when we say rule based, what we mean is that the process or activity follows a definite set of activities. Any deviations are based on some condition that are deterministic, can be evaluated, and are not subjective or based on any human judgement. The process or activity should have a standard operating procedure for execution.

Non disruptive

RPA is **non disruptive** and works along with the other applications in the IT ecosystem. RPA accesses the other applications in the eco system in a controlled manner with well-defined access and authority and does not require programmable changes in the business applications themselves. The existing architectural and governance policies can possibly be implemented with the bots, thus forming the integrated virtual workforce.

Benefits of Robotic Process Automation

The benefits achieved by the Robotic Process Automation can broadly be classified into three groups, as shown in the following diagram:

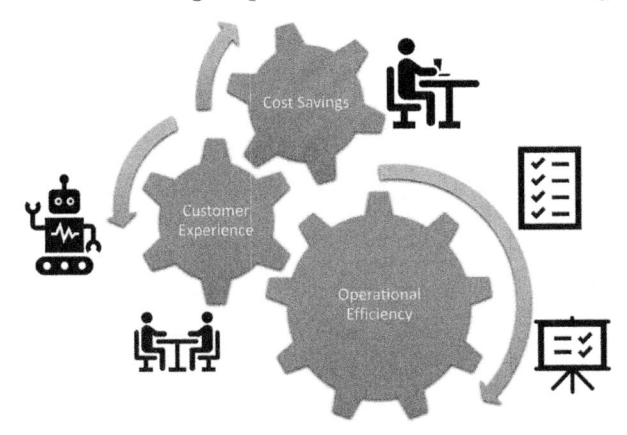

Figure 2.2: *Benefits of Robotic Process Automation*

These broad groups can further be broken down into individual value additions that the automation by RPA brings in. The following figure shows the benefits at a further granular level and indicates how they are aligned to the broader benefits:

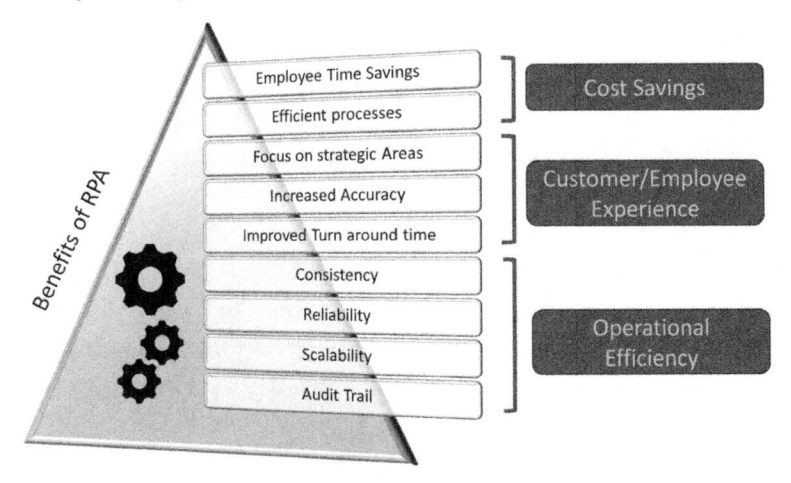

Figure 2.3: *Benefits of RPA*

Many of these benefits listed in the preceding figure are intertwined. Each of them might impact one another and contribute to the overall benefit of automation by RPA.

In the following few sections, we will discuss each of these benefits in the context of a sample scenario or use case.

Employee time savings

Automating the repetitive tasks saves time and money. Through RPA, as a bot mimics a human interaction with a system for a task, the employee is freed up to focus on higher valued tasks. Let's take an example where in the IT operations, the employees daily check the health of the different applications and databases. All they need to do is open the application and click on the different links or execute some standard commands to check if the application or database is up and running. This activity could take anywhere between 10-20 minutes on an average. If this is to be repeated across 100+ applications, imagine the amount of manual effort that is required daily, not mentioning the monotony and low enthusiasm of the employee. Automating such tasks and activities with RPA not only frees up the employee time, it also lets them focus on the more value-added tasks like analyzing the application problems and boosts the employee morale.

Similarly, in a Customer Inquiry or Complaint Management business process, the agent has to first read an email with the inquiry request or complaint and log a ticket to handle the issue and response back to the customer. There are two parts to it – (1) creating a ticket from the email, and (2) resolving the issue the customer is asking. The first part is a very repetitive process and, if automated, this would free up the agent's time and allow them to focus on building the customer relationship with an actual communication. The second part, if also repeatable, could very well be automated through RPA, provided the actions to resolve the issue is deterministic.

Improved Process Efficiency

Automation by RPA often has a positive impact on the process efficiency. Think of a scenario where there may be a need to collate the data from different sources and applications and then key in the consolidated data into a different back-office system. For example, in fraud analysis in Banking and Insurance, a wide variety of data might need to be consolidated from the different systems, both external and internal like profile, transaction history, identity data, credit ratings and so on. This collation and consolidation are labor intensive and need significant effort from the employees before they can actually analyze the data. An automated data consolidation by RPA to pull in the data from the different applications, which can then be analyzed by a human agent will make the process more efficient.

Increased accuracy and reduced human errors

A study by Forrester commissioned by UiPath in 2017, titled *The New Frontier Of Automation: Enterprise RPA* states that over 62% of the participants in the study, who are managerial or department level heads, expect that the reduction in errors will be one of the significant impacts of the RPA. Consider the scenarios in which an employee must do data entry which involves copying the data from multiple screens of different applications into a back-office system. Such an activity could typically be error prone. In many e-commerce scenarios, the customer order from the web channel may have to be keyed into the supplier's fulfilment application manually. As we are humans, there is a good probability for us to make errors. However, that might cause an increase in the cycle time of the order and customer dissatisfaction for the e-commerce player. Automation would reduce the human errors, and also increase the process efficiency.

Better turn around time

Turn Around Time or cycle time is the time taken to complete a process. This is one of the significant benefits of automation by RPA. Consider a use case in the IT Operations, where the monitoring system creates an alert when an application or node is going down. In a traditional scenario, there would be an agent eyeballing the monitoring dashboard, and once the event happens, the agent would be creating a ticket for the remediation. The ticket would then be assigned to the respective teams who would resolve the ticket and bring the application up again. A cycle time of such a Severity 1 ticket would be anywhere between 1/2-4 hours. Consider the same scenario, with the RPA based automation. As the system goes down, the event could be captured by another bot or an interceptor component invoking the bot. The bot would then automatically create a ticket in the Ticket Management system and then fire another bot to resolve the error and bring the system up (assuming this was a common failure cause and a bot was already programmed to remediate the error). Once resolved, the bot would update the ticket and maintain the full audit trail. Such automation would bring down the turnaround time to a considerable extent. There is a good example of how DHFL Pramerica Life Insurance automated their process of delivering tax certificates to their customers and brought down the turnaround time from 3 days to 10 minutes.

(https://cio.economictimes.indiatimes.com/news/strategy-and-management/how-rpa-helped-dhfl-pramerica-life-insurance-to-automate-tat-operation-etcio-annual-conclave-19/68421590)

Employees can focus on more strategic tasks

When you have a large pool of human resources doing important but repetitive manual work, often the focus on strategic activities is missed. Consider a car dealer, who needs to find the best deal for a car for the customer, and therefore spends a lot of time consolidating the data and searching for the best deal across multiple systems. If a bot could be programmed to do all the data consolidation and bring up a list of cars based on the customers' requirements, the agent could focus on a more important aspect – negotiating with the customer. This would also mean that with such automation, the employees can focus on the more stimulating work instead of the mundane and repetitive work, thus leading to a better employee engagement, better retention, and less churn of employees.

Consistency

Since the bots are programmed to do specific tasks repeatably in a certain way and without any variations (unless programmed explicitly), there is a lot of consistency in the outcome. Since the bots can't make mistakes, there is no deviation from the way the task is supposed to be executed. This adds to the overall consistent outcome when the tasks and activities are performed by the bots. This can be compared to the erroneous scenarios made by humans, unintentionally, which negatively impacts the overall outcome of the tasks and the consistency of the outcome. However, the flip side is that there may be cases where a bot might fail if it encounters a condition that it is not programmed for.

Reliability

When compared to the human employees, the bots are more reliable. The bots can be made available 24X7 to execute the tasks/activities that they are programmed for. As they are technological components, the bots can be deployed and configured in such a way that they are always available, if there is a business need. For example, just like the way we design the High Availability of the core applications, the associated software components of the bots can be deployed in a similar manner to address any failures that may arise during the operations.

Audit Trail

The bots can be programmed in such a way that there is a fully traceable audit trail available for the actions and tasks that a bot might execute. In doing so, not only do we achieve compliance, but there is a full traceability as well. When dealing with private data, the bots may provide a more secure handling of the data as opposed to the human agents with a suitable auditability built in. This is important, since we would like to know what changes the bots are making to our data and processes. There is still some apprehension around exposing the core business functions with private or sensitive data to the bots, but having a fully traceable audit trail can help in mitigating those apprehensions.

Scalability

Many a times, it might happen that due to a sudden increase or decrease in workload (predicted or unpredicted), there may be a need to scale up or scale down the resources. Take the Covid times for instance; in many industries like retail, there is a significant slump, leading to job losses. With the bots automating some of the supply chain processes, this shift in sales could be accommodated better for the automatable processes. Both the instances can be scaled up or down as per the load and volumetric associated with the process.

In the preceding sections, we discussed the potential benefits that RPA can achieve. However, it is important to understand that one of the key factors of successful benefit realization is the appropriate selection of the processes/activities to be automated. If the right process is selected for automation, the chances of realization of the benefits are higher. So, in the following section, let us understand what makes certain processes better suited for RPA based automation, and what are the factors that we should keep in mind when we are selecting the processes/use cases for the RPA based automation.

What makes a process fit for Robotic Process Automation

So far, we discussed about the different processes and use cases and the benefits that can be achieved by automating them through Robotic Process Automation.

In *Chapter 1, Introduction to Intelligent Automation*, we have learned that there are different levers of automation, and RPA is one of them. Now, let us understand what are the different criteria that a process should have to consider RPA as the best fit lever for its automation.

As we discussed in the previous sections, the RPA based automation has some key characteristics. The processes that can be automated by RPA need to have a series of documented steps, any variation/decision must be based on rules, and since it is a programmable software, the process needs to be executed in a digital environment.

Let us now understand the characteristics that a process should have to make it suitable for automation by RPA.

The characteristics of a process can be broadly classified into two categories – technical characteristic and non-technical characteristics – as shown in the following figure:

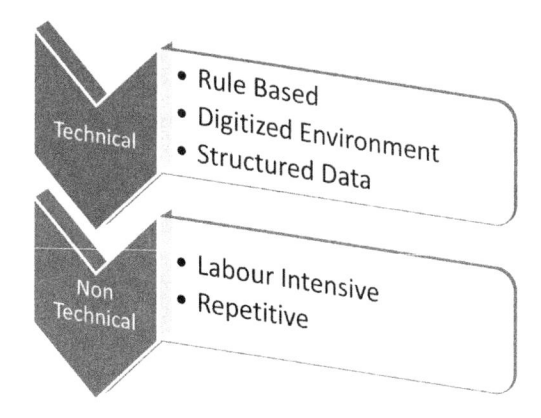

Figure 2.4: RPA Fitment Characteristics of a process

Technical Characteristics of Process required for RPA based Automation

This term "**rule based**" that we repeated many times, can be a little tricky to interpret. We have met with many process SMEs during various interactions with the teams, who have said that their processes are completely rule based. But when we went for a deeper analysis, it was found that there were several instances of human judgements and decisions that were taken intuitively and were not based on any documented rule in any form – be it digital or on paper. And this is very common. We humans are gifted with a powerhouse called brain which can process the information and derive decisions based on numerous criteria. It is almost impossible to replicate a human brain. The best AI machine could probably not even be half as intelligent as the human brain, ever. When assessing the fitment of a process for RPA, we need to clearly understand to what extent the process is rule based. This should also include the error and exception scenarios in addition to the happy path. So, the process to be automated by RPA should be based on documented rules with a deterministic outcome, clearly laying down the tasks that need to be performed in a sequence. This is an important technical criteria for a process to be automated by RPA.

It is also important to understand that RPA cannot take decisions or derive insights by itself. So, the rules are basically the drivers, that tell the RPA bots what tasks to execute, when to execute, and how to execute. Since the RPA bot is nothing but a programmable software, the rule-based criteria make it feasible for it to be a programmable software.

The second criterion that makes a process suitable for RPA from a technical perspective is that the process should operate in a *completely digitized environment,* i.e., all the tasks and activities in the process should be executed through some computer system and the digitized data should flow between the systems. This could be data entry / data updates in various systems, User Interface based application usage, or it could be a process which is triggered by a digital event like alerts, errors etc. The data available on printed, scanned, or handwritten documents may be unsuitable for processing by RPA. Since we are trying to automate the actions of a human operating on the different computer applications, it is a given that the whole processes should be executed in a digital environment.

The third technical criterion that makes a process fit for RPA implementation is the nature of the data it operates on. As discussed earlier, RPA is rule based and for the RPA implementation, the process also needs to follow a set of rules. However, these rules and the nature of the data that the process operates on needs to be structured. What

I mean by that is, the data should be in a pre-defined template or a defined data model and should be straight forward to analyze. Today, the pure vanilla RPA is not capable of interpreting and manipulating the unstructured data sets. RPA can be appended with technologies like **Optical Character Recognition (OCR)** and **Natural Language Processing (NLP)** to convert the unstructured data sets to structured data sets and make it suitable for RPA to act upon.

Non-Technical Characteristics of Process required for RPA based Automation

There are a few other characteristics of the process which are important to be considered for the RPA automation, and they contribute to the business fitment of the RPA based automation.

The main non-technical characteristics that we need to consider is that the process/activity to be automated should be **labor intensive**. This means that there should be a significant amount of labor savings that can be achieved by automating this process.

This can be broken down into a few sub factors.

The process should be **repetitive** in nature – the same work must be done by the human pool of workers multiple times a day/month/year.

The process should have a moderate to high cycle time and effort to complete the activities.

A simple calculation to find the labor intensity could be as follows:

$$Labor\ Intensity = (frequency * effort)/volume$$

This may not be the most precise calculation, but in most processes, this will give a fair idea to compare and quantify the labor intensity.

Apart from considering repetitiveness in the context of labor intensity, repetitiveness can also be considered in isolation. There may be a scenario where a process may need a small effort but is repeated every day; such a process will still need to be considered as a candidate process for the RPA based automation, and it may not be from a savings perspective, but more from an accuracy or process efficiency perspective.

So, to summarize, the preceding five broad characteristics – **Rule based**, Operates in **Digitized Environment**, Operates on **Structured**

Data, is **Labour Intensive,** and **Repetitive** in nature should be assessed for in a process to decide its fitment for the RPA based automation.

Now once we have shortlisted the candidate processes, we need to prioritize the processes for RPA.

For this, we need to consider the following three factors which contribute to the overall Return on Investment (RoI):

Automatability: This can be defined as the % of steps/tasks in a process that can be automated by RPA. Higher the %, the better automatability the process will have. It might happen that some steps may not be automated at all, or there may be some steps which could be automated by the other levers like AI.

Complexity: This would be the level of complexity of the process to be automated in terms of the number of steps, number of interfacing applications, processing complexity etc.

Benefits: This is a key measure to quantify the benefits of automation. Typically, this is measured in terms of FTE savings. However, there can be the other tangible benefits like increased accuracy, improved turnaround time etc.

The preceding three factors together can give a good indication of which processes should be prioritized for the RPA based automation.

However, we need to keep in mind that the RPA based automation is not a silver bullet to solve all the process woes. Unless the process is efficient and optimized, RPA can achieve limited benefits. If needed, process improvement and process reengineering complemented by process mining (will be discussed later in the book) can precede RPA automation to gain the most benefits.

Applicability of Robotic Process Automation through examples

Now that we understand what kind of processes are best fit for the RPA based automation, let us understand a few typical use cases for them.

In the following sections, we have tried to cover some indicative use cases from different industries and domains. This is a small indicative list – not exhaustive at all. This may or may not be completely automated by RPA, but it would be good to reflect on what makes them a good candidate process for RPA. We will refer to some of these use cases as we discuss the other technology levers in the coming chapters.

Financial Crime

In financial institutions like banks, there is an important function to detect and prevent financial crimes, frauds etc. This is a very important part of the business and is often mandated by government regulations. In this function, often, there is a team of people who monitor and check different the reports and a large volume of financial transactions to monitor and report suspicious activities. A part of this job requires gathering the data from different sources and then compiling them together in a report that will be further analyzed by the experts. The RPA bots can help extract (structured data) and collate the data, thus saving significant man hours.

Core Banking

Core banking includes the core banking functions around current and savings accounts in a banking institution.

Account Closure: Banks have a high volume of account closures and one of the reasons is that the customers fail to submit the mandatory documents. In such a scenario, tracking such customer accounts and sending them automatic notifications and reminders is an easy use case for RPA. There are a host of other automation use cases in Core Banking around the account servicing transactions – we will discuss them later as we proceed through the book.

Finance and Accounting

The Finance and Accounting process area is one of the low hanging fruits when it comes to RPA based automation. Some of the use cases are as follows:

Invoice processing: We discussed this in detail in *Chapter 1, Introduction to Intelligent Automation* as plain vanilla RPA use case and some enhancements for an Intelligent Automation use case.

Invoice creation: This process needs the data from the CRM system and the Accounting System. The RPA bots can pull in the data from the relevant CRM and Billing systems and successfully generate the invoices.

Account reconciliation: Account reconciliation requires consolidation of data from various systems including customer invoices, spreadsheets, accounting systems. RPA can be instrumental in such reconciliation use cases.

Take a look at the following diagram to understand the process of account reconciliation and reflect on how RPA is a good fit for automating the same :

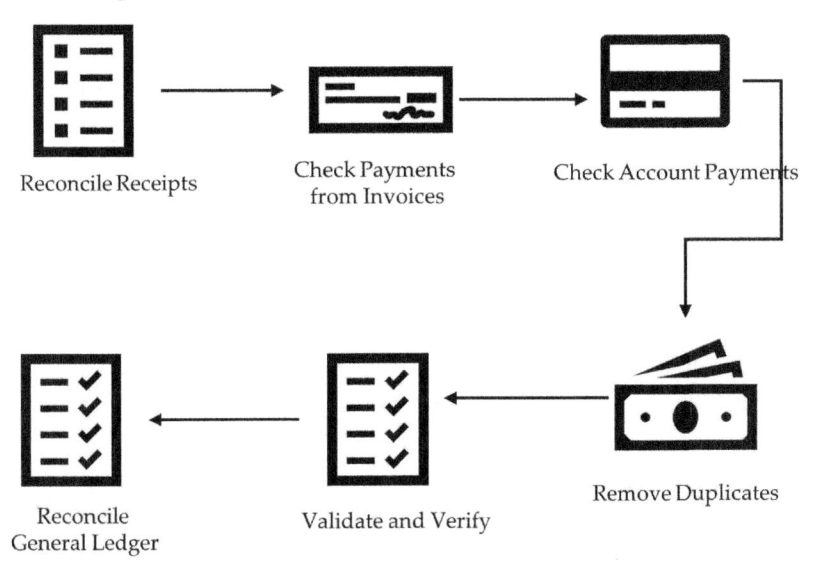

Figure 2.5: *Account Reconciliation*

Procurement

There are a lot of use cases in the back-office operations as we saw in Finance and Accounting. Procurement is another area where there are a lot of repeatable activities that can be a good fit for the RPA based automation. Some of the use cases are as follows:

Creating Sales Orders: Typically, the sales representative need to create the sales orders in a CRM system. Downstream, there could be a fulfilment system and the sales order needs to be copied into the other downstream system. Being a manual and repetitive work, this could be a good fit for an RPA use case.

In procurement, there are many such use cases that can be implemented with RPA and generate significant benefits. Price tracking and selecting the best price for a part is usually a very laborious process. This includes checking the price for the parts from different vendors and selecting the best price. The data is available in different formats and from different sources. RPA can monitor and check the different prices and select the best price based on the business rules.

Scheduling and Tracking Shipments: This is also a laborious process where you schedule the shipment, and for tracking and monitoring, you might need to access the vendor portals. An RPA bot can efficiently do this and report back when the tracking is complete.

In the processes involving waivers, refunds are also good use cases for RPA, since in most cases, they are based on distinct business rules, and operate on structured data between the systems.

Customer/Vendor Management

Customer and Vendor Managements are core processes in most Enterprise Resource Planning and Customer oriented processes.

Maintain the CRM system data: Usually, the CRM system should have the data regarding all the customer communications/interactions. Many a times, the agents have to manually pull in the data from the chats, emails, etc., to update the CRM system. In case of templatized emails and chats, this could be a pure RPA use case, creating a one-stop shop for all the customer data.

Vendor Record Management: A similar use case for consolidating all vendor data with a bot doing the data consolidation could be an Updating Vendor data use case.

Patient Management in Healthcare

In any visit to a hospital or clinic, we typically have to start off with giving the patient details before we can connect with a doctor. Such processes are at the core of Patient Management systems in healthcare.

Scheduling Patient Appointments in Healthcare centers: The bots can help in scheduling the appointments based on the customer profile, nature of appointment, diagnosis, location, availability of doctor, and many other criteria as required.

Payroll in HR

Processing the payroll is a laborious process that must be repeated every month or every pay cycle. This process needs a huge amount of data consolidation effort from the various systems across the enterprise and the external systems as well. Using RPA for consolidating the data across the multiple systems, validating the data against the organizations policies for benefits, reimbursements, loans, lease, leave etc., and finally creating the payment can be a great use case to automate for the HR department. This will not only result in FTE reductions, but also make the process error free and increase the employees' delight with timely pay checks.

The other significant use cases in HR could be the onboarding of new hires and offboarding of employees. Both the processes include gathering the data and updating them in the various enterprise systems; there are completely repetitive and rule-based work.

Generic use cases

Apart from Industry and domain specific use cases, the following are some generic usecases that are prevalent and common across business processes.

Data validations between systems: The RPA-enabled automation to verify and validate the different types of data by fetching the inputs from multiple third-party applications is a significant use case.

Maker Checker processes: The bot can enter the relevant data with the profile of a maker and submit in the system. Once this is done, the same bot can log in with the profile of a checker, validate the request, and approve.

Take a look at the following diagram for an understanding of the Maker Checker process and reflect on the usage of RPA to automate the process:

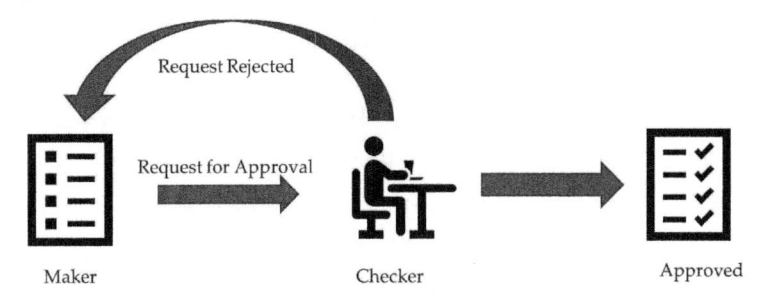

Figure 2.6: Maker Checker Process

IT Operations use cases

IT Operations is one of the areas where we see lot of automation opportunities. Some typical use cases are listed below.

Software Installations, Patch Management: RPA is well suited for usage in regular software installations and patch updates, which are extremely routine, rule based, and repetitive across the enterprise.

Report Data Aggregation and Report creation: Aggregating the data from disparate systems and creating reports are a regular activity in most enterprises. This requires significant manual effort and being repetitive and operating on structured data from the enterprise systems of record; this type of report generation use cases are very well suited for RPA automation.

User Set up and Configuration: A New User set up in an enterprise or even in a specific project context usually involves a set up and configuration of the different enterprise software, platform, and tools. Post the installation, an employee would need access to the different set to tools and software platforms which can also be done by RPA.

Application and Database Health Checks: This is a typical non-ticketing activity that the IT Operations team usually performs regularly. This involves checking whether the application is up and running and verifying that the key functionalities are working by clicking on the different links/buttons and other controls. Similarly, for the database health checks, the operations team member must check for the available disk space, available memory, size of transaction logs etc., and verify that they are within the safe thresholds. All of these are activities that can easily be automated by RPA and would not only result in cost savings but also enable the resources to focus on the more intellectually stimulating work.

User Management: User Management usually involves creating and managing the new users and their access to the different enterprise systems like applications, databases, networks, storage systems, SaaS services, and so on. These activities broadly fit most of the criteria of RPA automation. Password reset is one of the most common use cases that I have seen getting automated as a start to the RPA journey.

Data migration: RPA can be extremely effective in automating the data migration activities. Since these would be very rule based, it would be a good fit for the RPA based automation, which would also save the manual labor that is usually required for such activities.

Alert Monitoring: Do you remember the example we discussed in *Chapter 1, Introduction to Intelligent Automation*, about how RPA could be used for auto remediation of alerts? Alert monitoring and remediation are a popular and efficient use case for RPA. Typically, we do ticket analytics in matured enterprises and can identify the problem areas where the maximum tickets occur, or which type of tickets take the most amount of time to resolve. Depending on the automation priorities, RPA can be used to resolve the root cause. The only point to remember here is that the resolution for which the bot is being programmed, should be a deterministic and proven resolution. Otherwise, it might need AI, first to predict the recommended resolution and then for executing the action.

Level 1 and Level 2 Ticket Resolution: Similar applicability of RPA is there in the entire Ticket Management and Resolution area of the IT Operations. This is one of the prime areas where most enterprises have already started the RPA based automation. Runbook is very common in the IT operations. It is a document that describes the processes on how to execute the commonly occurring IT tasks. Many organizations, that I have seen, have started their automation with Runbook automation – this means, they have automated the tasks mentioned in the Runbook, based on the existing documented tasks, thus automating a good portion of the commonly recurring IT tasks. We will discuss the ticket resolution use case in detail in *Chapter 5 : Intelligent Automation Use cases*, later in the book.

In the preceding section, we have seen many different use cases, both from business and IT operations, which have a strong affinity to be automated by RPA. However, it is important to understand that these are only indicative use cases. In real engagements, there will be a lot more, depending on what functional areas are being assessed for automation. Depending on the industries and domains, the nature and description of the processes would also change. The reason for mentioning these processes here is to give you a clear idea about the various kind of processes, that would be good for the RPA based automation, and about what would be a few common use cases in the various industries.

Preferred practices

Just like any other technology implementation project, the RPA projects are no different. It needs planning and preparation and, most importantly, a clear vision of the RPA journey. In the following few sections, we will discuss the various phases of an RPA delivery lifecycle. RPA development is no different from any other IT Development project. So, in the next few pages, as we discuss the different phases of development, we will focus only on those areas, that are specific and slightly different for the RPA delivery. For example, in Testing, we will discuss what the additional considerations for RPA bot testing are, and not discuss on-the-whole testing lifecycle like creating test plans, test data, execution of scripts, and tracking them to completion.

The following diagram shows the broad phases in a typical RPA delivery Lifecycle:

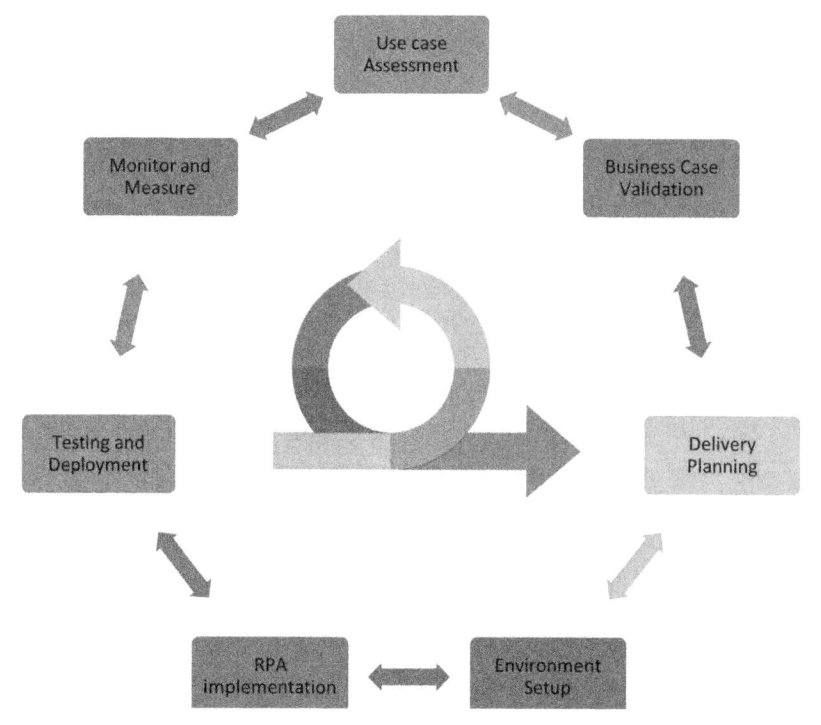

Figure 2.7: Delivery Lifecycle of RPA project

Use Case Identification and Assessment

The first phase for an RPA implementation or, for that matter, any automation implementation is identifying the use case. As we discussed earlier, we should select a process/activity for the RPA implementation by assessing the technical and non-technical criteria together. This assessment will ensure that not only are we selecting a process that is appropriate for the RPA implementation from a technical feasibility aspect, but also that the process has a significant automation potential and RoI.

In several instances, we have heard the automation leaders say that they have implemented RPA but have not achieved the expected benefits. One of the reasons behind such a statement can be attributed to the use case selection. If the use case is selected purely based on the technology fitment, overlooking the business justification, we are bound to get into such scenarios.

Another important aspect of this identification process is to include both, the business and the IT teams together for these discussions. The different stakeholders of a process/activity from the business and IT may have different perspectives, addressing which is very critical for the successful adoption of RPA. Hence, combining the technical and business aspect along with their respective representation during the use case identification is one of the most critical steps in the whole RPA delivery cycle.

Business Case Validation

This is a logical extension once the appropriate use case has been identified. The use case needs to be analyzed, breaking it down into smaller activities and tasks. The volumetric, total effort required for the use case needs to be identified and analyzed. The idea in this step is to quantify the benefits and calculate the total cost of ownership of the RPA automation, which would then be documented in a Business Case and presented for validation to the approving authority.

Delivery Project Planning and Kick off

Once the business case is validated, typically that means that you have received a go-ahead to start the delivery of the selected RPA automation development. This phase is a typical planning phase, where the entire project plan and work breakdown structure needs to be created. A delivery methodology like Agile may be selected and, based on that, the different milestones and deliverables can be defined.

Environment Preparation

This is an important phase and planning for the environment should have started long before, during the use case identification step in all probability. The RPA environment set up might need some significant time, effort, and capital investment, in terms of procuring the hardware and software licenses and set up. The different RPA tools available in the market have different specifications and license costs. Depending on the number of bots you plan to scale up to, this can be defined and planned accordingly. This will be a one-time activity and an important prerequisite to starting the next step – the implementation.

RPA implementation

Implementation phase typically includes design, development, testing and deployment of the software.

Design and Development: This phase typically starts with creating the process design – where each task in the identified use case is detailed out, capturing the steps a human user would execute, checking for the applications that is interfaced, business rules being triggered, and the data entered or updated. This is the phase where you are designing the automata to be executed. Some important considerations at this stage would be modularity and reusability of the flow, exception handling, logging, and auditability – all of which will make the RPA program easy to maintain and enhance. In some cases, it might also happen that there may be a need to improve or standardize the process. In such a situation, the ground rule is to automate the best process instead of a faulty, inefficient process. So sometimes, we might need to focus on process improvement before proceeding to the process design for bot development.

The development activities in this phase happen in the RPA tool specific development environments, studios, IDEs etc., that are usually a part of the RPA tool framework. In many tools, there are user friendly, drag-and-drop kind of mechanism available to configure and create the activity blocks, tasks, rules, mark interfaces, add business logic, and so on. Depending on the tool of choice, there would be defined steps for packaging the coded programs for deployment. These will be developed based on the micro design or system design that is specified during the system design activity. The latest in RPA development includes low code platforms that can be used by business users to create the bots. We will touch upon this briefly in *Chapter 7: Intelligent Automation – Trends and Future*.

Testing and Deployment: Once the RPA automata has been developed, it needs to be tested before deployment. What becomes very important in the RPA testing, is availability of a production like environment or a pre-production system. This is because the RPA automata will work on the live enterprise systems – say, it will act on the CRM system to add data, or the Billing system to do reconciliation. In both the cases, the availability of a production like instance of the CRM or Billing system, with the right kind of data is very important, for the adequate testing of RPA to be done.

In many situations, we have seen that the availability of such a pre-production environment with the right kind of data is often a challenge. This should be raised during the project planning phase, and plans should be made to make it available during the testing to make the implementation successful. The deployment of RPA is typically done following the RPA Tool specific deployment instructions.

Monitor and measure

Post the deployment, as the RPA automation goes live, there are two aspects that we need to consider. One is the monitoring part – where just like any other live system, we might need to monitor the deployed bots for any failure or errors. In a small scale, this may be managed by the existing pool of resources, but as the automation in the enterprise scales up, there may be a need of automated monitoring.

The second aspect is to measure the benefits. This is one of the most important activities in the whole RPA delivery lifecycle. Remember, during the identification of use case, we quantified the benefits that will be achieved by automating the process/activity? That quantified number needs to be measured and validated now and this might lead to more requirements for enhancing the current automation or identifying the peripheral automation requirements of the activity/process under consideration.

So far, we have discussed the RPA delivery method, touching upon some of the key factors which we should consider during an RPA implementation. However, it is important to keep in mind, that the preceding method and phase descriptions should not be followed in isolation. These are on top of the usual IT development and delivery best practices that we typically follow – capture "SMART" requirements, both functional and non-functional, decoupled, and cohesive design, modularity and flexibility built in, and testing – following the best practices and so on to achieve the desired results of following a structure method for delivery.

Bot or API

Should I use RPA to execute my tasks and activities, or should I use an API? We have heard questions on this many a times in different forums – right from the IT Directors to the developer. Probably while reading this chapter, this question might have arisen in your minds too.

My answer is typical of an architect, that it would depend on the context. RPA, as you have seen by now, is very good at mimicking human actions, interacting with different application front ends, clicking, copying data, and so on. APIs are the integration mechanism between multiple applications through a defined and published interface. In the long run, APIs are lower in cost of ownership than the RPA in most cases. However, API based integration between two systems might be a larger effort than a quick RPA.So, the best usage of these two powerful levers of automation would be a combination based on the fitment. For example, if APIs are available for say, creating a purchase order, then RPA could be leveraged in the initial part of the process, during the capture of the data. RPA could copy the data from a spreadsheet in which it is originally found in the enterprise, cleanse and consolidate the data as needed, and then call the API to execute the transaction and store it in the back-office system. It is important to understand that there is no conflict of interest between an RPA bot and API. Both are efficient levers of automation. The appropriate usage should be decided keeping the overall process/activity and the automation strategy in mind, along with any security consideration, hosting impacts, and overall cost of ownership.

Products and tools

This chapter will not be complete if we don't touch upon the various RPA tools available today in the market. The RPA technology and associated ecosystem has evolved and matured quite a lot in the recent years. In fact, there are several product vendors, who have come up with the AI infused RPA bots which can accelerate the journey to the Intelligent Automation.

Broadly, there can be the following three categories of RPA bots:

Attended bots: The bots that require human intervention to complete the automation.

Unattended bots: The bots that complete the end-to-end activity without manual intervention.

Hybrid or mixed bots: The bots that can combine the capabilities of both the attended and the unattended bots.

Depending on the process to be automated and the capabilities of the RPA tool, we can decide what type of bots will be best suited for the implementation.

RPA tools

There are numerous RPA tools in the market today. Based on the analyst's recommendation, a few have emerged as market leaders. In this bookwe will not do any comparisonof any RPA products or explain in detail any specific tool capabilities. The product websites have very rich content that can be leveraged for that.

Usually, we have have tool evaluation methodologies which can be followed to decide the tool of choice, based on the nature of the use cases to be automated. There is a plethora of resources on the internet, providing guidance and comparisons for the same.

The following figure is based on a Forrester research from Q4 2019:

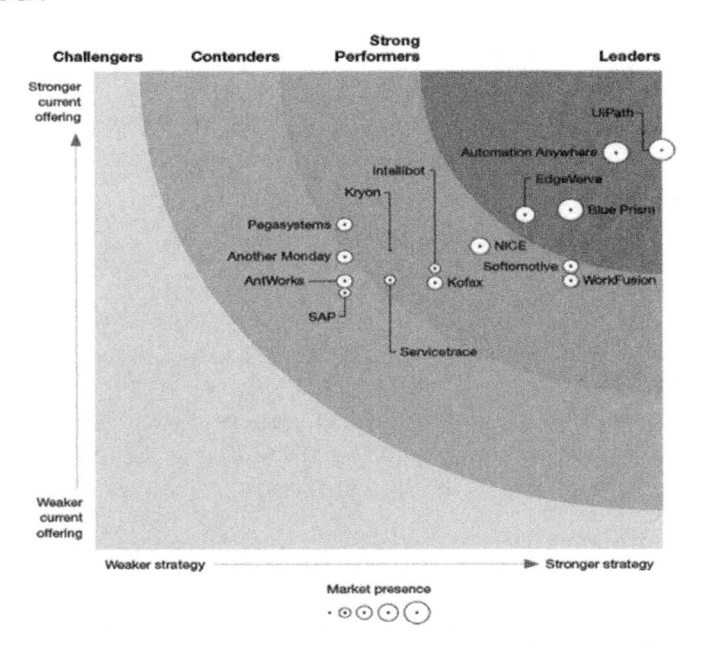

Figure 2.8: *Forrester View on Robotic Process Automation Vendors -2019. Source: www.forrester.com*

Please refer to the Forrester website for the latest 2021 view.

(https://www.gartner.com/en/documents/3988021/magic-quadrant-for-robotic-process-automation)

Robotic Process Automation or RPA thus remains an important lever in the overall Intelligent Automation space. There are many products and tools available, and the evaluation of the tool's capabilities against the organizations' RPA requirements need to be done, while selecting a tool of choice. Apart from comparing the functional capabilities, some other important comparison criteria could be scalability, as a service availability, availability of the AI features if needed, performance (on online applications, desktop application, Citrix applications), development effort, ease of use/configuration would be important considerations while selecting a tool. These would impact the overall delivery, performance, and management of the RPA automation.

Another important point that we want to touch upon here is that in today's organizations with complex processes and business models, it might happen that selecting one RPA tool may not suffice. In such a case, a combination of different tools would add to the overall automation portfolio of the enterprise.

Conclusion

In this chapter, we understood what Robotic Process Automation is and how RPA contributes as a key component in the automation landscape.

To summarize, Robotic Process Automation or RPA are programmable software components that can be used to mimic the human actions and activities on different application systems to complete a process or activity. RPA works best on the processes that are repetitive, rule based, works on structured data, and are available in a digital environment. To achieve the full benefit from the RPA based automation, the processes selected should be labor intensive with a significant volume and repetitive in nature.

In this chapter, we discussed a lot of indicative use cases across the different industries and domains to get an idea about the things that RPA can do and the benefits it can bring. We also discussed the RPA delivery method and understood the different phases and the important considerations in each phase. Lastly, we touched upon a snapshot of the various RPA tools available in the market.

We would like to leave you with this thought in mind that RPA is a very powerful and integral component of automation now. When used in conjunction with the other levers of automation like Integration and AI, it can accelerate the enterprise's journey towards Intelligent Automation.

In the next chapter, *Chapter 3, Artificial Intelligence in Automation*, we will see how this foundational automation is augmented with AI to build Intelligent Automation.

Reference

1. Will robots steal our jobs? **https://www.weforum.org/agenda/2019/08/the-robots-are-coming-but-take-a-breath**

2. New Frontier of Automation – Enterprise RPA - **https://www.uipath.com/resources/automation-analyst-reports/future-of-employees-rpa-forrester-report**

3. How RPA helped DHFL Pramerica Life Insurance :

    https://cio.economictimes.indiatimes.com/news/strategy-and-management/how-rpa-helped-dhfl-pramerica-life-insurance-to-automate-tat-operation-etcio-annual-conclave-19/68421590

CHAPTER 3
Artificial Intelligence in Automation

Introduction

In Intelligent Automation, as the name indicates, Artificial Intelligence is the key element that makes the automation intelligent. It is the Artificial Intelligence that transforms the automation from being reactive to proactive, from being driven by rules to being driven by intelligence. If we see the recent reports on the future of technology by the **World Economic Forum (WEF)**, there is a predominance of focus on AI and how it can be leveraged in various industries. In one of the reports, it states how Artificial Intelligence is going to be one of the key drivers of the *Fourth Industrial Revolution* and automation is one of the imperatives that will leverage this AI wave with intelligent automation.

In today's world, with Intelligent Automation, AI is infused in processes, operations, and experience. Intelligent Automation has thus become an overall enabler in the business fueled by AI.

As we move ahead from task automation to process automation, not only do we want the tasks and activities to be automated, but we also want the process to become smart, to be able to sense and respond to the interactions and react, based on the circumstances or conditions, and all of these, without being explicitly programmed for. That is the essence of Intelligent Automation. And as you might have realized by now, many of these capabilities that are needed to build an intelligent and proactive automation go beyond the rules-driven automation and need AI.

In this chapter, we will discuss and understand Artificial Intelligence as a driver of Intelligent Automation, how it impacts and transforms automation, the benefits it can bring, and how to plan and start such an AI-driven automation journey in an enterprise.

Structure

In this chapter, we will cover the following topics:

- Purpose of AI in Automation
- Types of AI in Automation
- Benefits of AI
- Best suited AI use cases
- AI Best practices
- AI Frameworks and product

Objective

After reading this chapter, you will be able to understand the importance of Artificial Intelligence in implementing Intelligent Automation. You will also be able to understand and articulate how to infuse AI into broader automation landscape and the type of business benefits that can be achieved through that. This chapter will help you apply AI in automation through the various use cases and scenarios that we will discuss as we progress in the chapter. Focusing on how to deliver AI based automation, you will be able to understand and imbibe the best practices covering all the lifecycle phases – requirements, design, development, and testing. Since the technological discussions are rarely complete without having an idea about the products and frameworks around AI, we will end this chapter with the leading products that can help you build the AI solutions in Intelligent Automation.

Purpose of Artificial Intelligence in Automation

Artificial Intelligence can be defined as infusing human like intelligence into the machines and computer programs. Artificial Intelligence goes way back to 1950 when *Alan Turing* said that human brains are like computers – initially it's an *"unorganized machine"*, which through *"training"* becomes like a *"universal machine"* in *"Computer Machine and Intelligence"*. He proposed the *"Turing Test"* to determine whether a computer can *"think"*.

Broadly speaking, human intelligence can be made up of multiple components like learning, reasoning, problem solving, sense and perception, and language processing. Building these capabilities into the machines and computer programs results in Artificial Intelligence. In today's times, we can see these manifested as personal assistants like Siri or Alexa, Image recognition like Google Lens, virtual assistants or chatbots for business and consumer, recommendation engines, prediction tools, and so on.

We saw in *Chapter 2: Robotic Process Automation*, that RPA is one of the key levers of Intelligent Automation and it is very effective in automating the repetitive tasks. However, there are scenarios where RPA alone may not be able to automate the process. Requirements like decisioning, recommendation, interpretation and several others would need additional automation components like AI to achieve the end-to-end automation of the process.

With AI as a lever of automation, we can achieve another degree of automation with the automated and proactive detection of events, automated interpretation of the information, and automated decisions on what must be done and decide on the relevant actions to be taken.

Going back to the analogy of Intelligent Automation with the way humans function, if RPA can be considered as the limbs – arms and legs – that perform the actions like running or writing, we can consider AI as the brain that understands and decides what the limbs will do in a particular circumstance. Thus, true to its name, we can see that AI is *"the"* key component in making the automation intelligent.

Different types of AI in intelligent automation

In this chapter, we will discuss the various components of AI that are relevant and applicable for Intelligent Automation.

Today, we hear a lot of chatter about AI, ML, deep learning (DL), and the likes, in various contexts, sometimes even interchangeably. Let us try to understand the positioning of AI, ML, and DL briefly in very basic terms. Take a look at the following graphical representation on how AI, ML, and DL fit together:

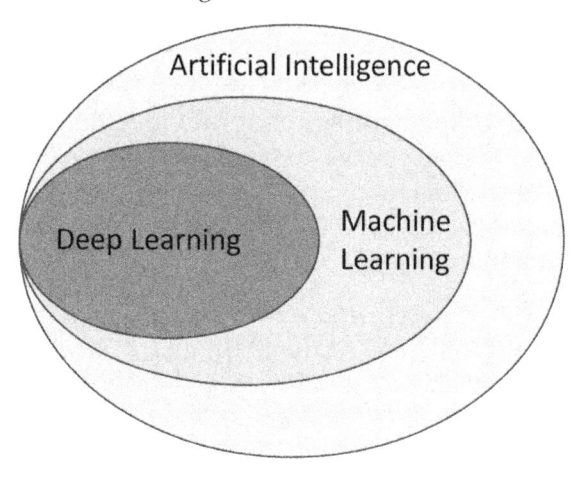

Figure 3.1: Artificial Intelligence, Machine Learning and Deep Learning – where they fit together

Artificial Intelligence is a broad area, where we develop computer systems to imitate human intelligence. This can include learning, problem solving, decision making, interpretation, identification and so on.

Machine Learning is a subset of Artificial Intelligence, which deals with building models and algorithms to perform specific tasks like prediction, recommendation, identification, and so on. This can be based on supervised or unsupervised learning.

Deep learning is a super specialization of machine learning, where algorithms can train themselves using neural networks exposed to huge volumes of data.

There are different frameworks available for each of the preceding areas, providing mechanisms to process and analyze the data and build the models and neural networks.

Going slightly deeper into machine learning, Machine Learning algorithms can broadly be classified into three categories – *supervised*, *unsupervised*, and *reinforced learning*.

In **supervised** learning, the system is imparted intelligence based on a set of data – with the inputs mapped to the outputs in the training dataset with the help of labels. It derives the function based on this labeled training data where we train the system with the input-output combination data. Supervised learning is usually used in a scenario when we know what we are looking for.

In **unsupervised** learning, the algorithm must derive the inference based on the input data without any mapped or labeled output corresponding to it. Unsupervised learning is more applicable in cases where we don't know what we are specifically looking for and need to conduct an exploration or a discovery.

Reinforced learning is a little different from both the supervised and the unsupervised learning. Supervised learning finds the best labeled data based on the data that it has been trained with. Unsupervised learning broadly groups the data into logical groups. In reinforced learning, the algorithm learns to react to an environment, getting rewarded for good actions, and learns based on that. It is more of a behavioral learning model and the system learns through trial and error. There is usually no labeled data set on which the system is trained.

There are different algorithms for each of the preceding type of machine learning and there is a plethora of resources in the public domain where you can get more information on the details of each of the algorithms.

A subset of machine learning is deep learning. This is a specialized stream of machine learning in which there are neural networks iteratively acting on the data to derive the knowledge. The data is usually unstructured and unlabeled. Deep learning is supposed to mimic the way a human brain works to identify the objects in the environment, understand the interactions through speech and languages, and make relevant decisions.

66 ■ *Intelligent Automation Simplified*

In *Figure 3.2*, there are a few common algorithms for each of the categories. It is not an exhaustive list and is meant to trigger your interest, so that you can go ahead and read more on each of these on your own. The key here from an Intelligent Automation perspective is the applicability of the algorithms in solving the different types of problems, where it fits, what kind of data collection mechanism you would need, and what would be the considerations in terms of hardware and software resources that you would need to deploy. Take a look at the following diagram to understand the categories of machine learning and associated algorithms:

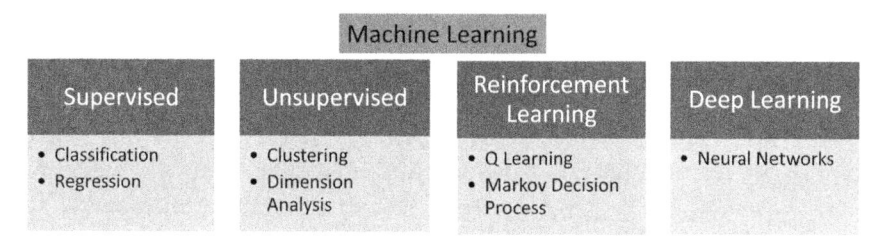

```
                        Machine Learning
┌──────────────┐  ┌──────────────┐  ┌──────────────┐  ┌──────────────┐
│  Supervised  │  │ Unsupervised │  │ Reinforcement│  │ Deep Learning│
│              │  │              │  │   Learning   │  │              │
├──────────────┤  ├──────────────┤  ├──────────────┤  ├──────────────┤
│• Classification│ │• Clustering │  │• Q Learning  │  │• Neural Networks│
│• Regression  │  │• Dimension   │  │• Markov Decision│              │
│              │  │  Analysis    │  │  Process     │  │              │
└──────────────┘  └──────────────┘  └──────────────┘  └──────────────┘
```

Figure 3.2: *Categories of Machine Learning*

The algorithm details are beyod the scope of this book. There are a lot of resources, online and offline, that you could leverage to gain a better understanding of these. In this chapter, from here on, we will discuss the applicability of some of these in Intelligent Automation.

In the context of Intelligent Automation, we have grouped the AI capabilities into four broad categories. In the following section, we will discuss each of these capabilities in detail. However, we will not dive deep into the algorithms, and only focus on the applicability of each of these in the context of automation. In the context of Intelligent Automation, a single capability, or any combination of capabilities from these categories, can be used and applied in automating the business processes.

Take a look at the following diagram to understand the categories of AI capabilities in Intelligent Automation:

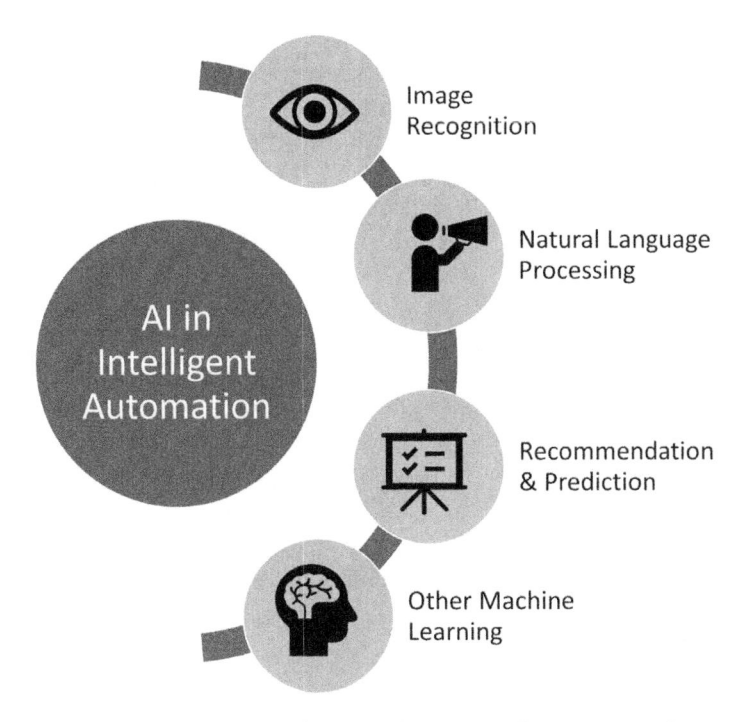

Figure 3.3: Categories of AI capabilities in Intelligent Automation

Image Recognition

Image recognition is the capability of a system to identify the images of the objects, places, things, or actions or anything, and categorize them. This type of AI system usually takes an image as the input. The image can be captured through any camera and be available as a digital input. Typically, to build the AI capabilities, we need a significant volume of data through which we can train the system for the required purpose. In this case, the AI system is fed with the images and trained with image recognition algorithms which interpret the image. The algorithm identifies the image based on the labels it has been trained on – like object, action, elements, place, and so on, along with a confidence score on the accuracy of recognition. The clarity and resolution of the image usually has an impact on the accuracy of the image recognition algorithm.

Image recognition is usually based on the deep learning algorithms. The deep learning algorithms use neural networks to build the algorithms that can identify the image.

A very simple example of image recognition, which has been very prevalent, is **Optical Character Recognition (OCR)**. The image of the text is usually the input, and the output is the text with the alphabets/numbers identified. For example, the input can be a license plate of a car, and the output would be the license plate number with the characters identified.

The advanced image recognition would include face recognition – like you see in the Android devices, or in the Facebook photo tagging in our regular lives. In a more business context, the image recognition could involve recognizing the machine parts for faults, identifying the different text/data from images, processing the images of various identity docs in the standard or non-standard formats, and so on. Image recognition has a varied type of usage in automation and can play an important part in achieving end to end automation in suitable use cases. Visual recognition, as already stated, involves specialized machine learning algorithms to identify the various images based on the training of the AI system.

Image recognition can include identifying a single image – say identifying a certain object in an image or it could include identifying multiple metadata about the image like location, objects, mood, and so on. Broadly, as mentioned in the previous section, the image or visual recognition solutions use the deep learning techniques to classify the image, recognize specific objects or track them, and retrieve images or generate them.

There are several image recognitions tools, products, open-source libraries providing APIs which provide the image recognition algorithms that can be used to build and train the custom models. *OpenCV, TensorFlow, Keras, Google Colab* are some of the popular open-source image processing solutions.

Let us now talk about implementation. To build an AI model, we need to define the specific problem and prepare a significantly large dataset to build and train the model. The following diagram shows a high-level sequence of the broad activities that are required to build an AI model, a visual or image recognition model in this case:

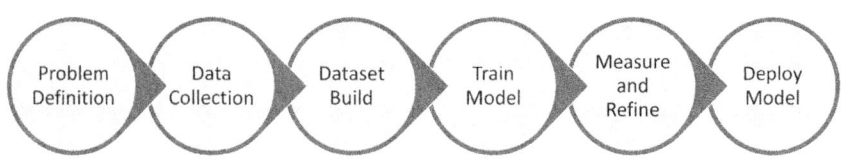

Figure 3.4: Phases of an Image recognition Model Project

These phases are mostly the same in any AI project's lifecycle. The data collection, preparation strategy, and activities may differ, the model train and build algorithms may differ, but broadly speaking, the activities remain the same. We will discuss these activities and the overall development methodology in a later section.

Natural Language Processing

Natural language processing (NLP) is the capability of an AI system to converse with a human in the way human communication usually occurs. This includes speaking naturally with a system without using any specific keywords to trigger the system, including colloquial terms, or writing with grammatical mistakes, acronyms, and colloquial expressions. This is widely used these days through conversational AI like chatbots and virtual assistants, where the interaction between a man and a machine is made to appear natural and seamless. Conversational AI is made up of multiple capabilities like natural language understanding, natural language processing to understand the intent, disambiguation if any, and finding the right response relevant to the conversation.

A key feature of matured conversational AI is that it can engage in a dialogue within a specific context. If I ask Alexa, *"how is the weather today"*, it can identify that I am in Delhi (based on my profile information) and will respond to me with the weather report of Delhi.

What makes the conversational AI conversational? Let us understand how this works. It starts with the user instantiating the conversation with a request – may be a question or an *"ask for guidance"*. The AI system can understand the intent of the question despite the way is it asked, its grammar, or the acronyms. It is important to understand that this interpretation is not based on any keywords or phrases. The AI system employs machine learning to understand the intent of the conversation and has been trained to interpret the intent. It then determines the right response and presents the response in a form that is usually used in human interactions. Usually, the conversational AI is implemented via chatbots and virtual assistants of different types.

In this context, it is important to appreciate the fact that not all chatbots are conversational AI systems. There could be some chatbots that are usually scripted with rules and keywords. These kind of chatbots are usually used for conversation on very specific areas and are programmed explicitly to understand the questions and navigate to the right answer. However, for these types of chatbots, it may get difficult to scale to new conversations.

Natural language processing is a huge field of study and has usage beyond chatbots. Sentiment Analysis is another AI capability where the natural language processing is used. Based on what we write, post, or speak, the AI systems can detect the major sentiments expressed in the conversation. This information can have various usage – if the AI system detects anger in a customer, it can direct to the smartest agent or offer products/freebies to ensure retention/prevent churn.

There are several natural language processing tools, products, and open-source libraries providing APIs, which provide the natural language processing algorithms that can be used to build and train the NLP models.

The high-level sequence of the broad activities that are required to build an NLP model is more or less similar to a visual recognition model building and includes similar activities – only in a different context, different data, and different measure.

Take a look at the following diagram to understand the high-level activities for building an NLP model:

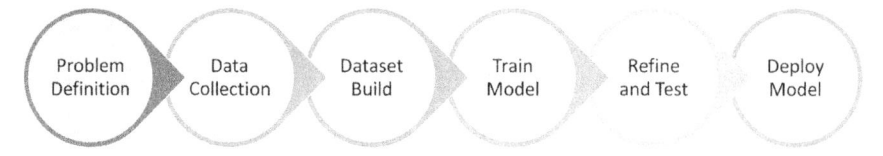

Figure 3.5: High Level Activities for building an NLP model

As you can see, the preceding diagram depicts the typical lifecycle phases of an AI project – be it image recognition, natural language processing, or others. We will discuss each of the phases and the activities done in each, when we discuss the AI Project lifecycle later in this chapter.

Recommendation and Prediction

A recommendation system is an AI system which suggests and recommends products, services, actions etc., based on the users' profile, behaviour, interests, transactions, and a host of other data, depending on the business problem. It does this by analyzing and modeling on the data based on the customer's behaviour and interactions.

The recommendation systems have been prevalent since a long time – probably the early 2000s, but now it has become almost a business imperative for many businesses.

The recommendation engines use the machine learning algorithms which are usually of two types – **content based filtering** and **collaborative filtering**. The content based filtering considers similarity between the products and their attributes to arrive at recommendations, while the collaborative filtering uses patterns in customer interactions. Many recommendation engines use a combination of the two to arrive at optimum results.

A recommendation engine creates the suggestions or recommendations based on a large amount of analysis of data. Hence, collecting the right type of data and building the data set is very important in building such a system. In this context, the data may be classified into implicit, like the transaction history of a specific user, his/her click stream data etc., or explicit, like the ratings or comments given by the user.

Largely, a recommendation system would have a typical cycle for the development which includes the collection of relevant data, data storage, data analysis at real time, near real time, or in batch, and finally filtering the data to generate the recommendation model based on the most appropriate algorithm – collaborative, content based, or a combination. The lifecycle is the same as for the ones we discussed earlier; we will delve deeper into them later in this chapter.

Other Machine Learning

The preceding capabilities are well known and are the common AI capabilities that are very relevant in the context of Intelligent Automation. However, we need to understand that this is not an exhaustive list. There are other types of AI services which are analytical, functional, or textual in nature, and various other algorithms for a variety of requirements. Depending on the nature of automation that we want to achieve in a scenario or a use case, a combination of these different types of AI services will be applied.

Benefits of Artificial Intelligence in Automation

The benefits achieved by Artificial Intelligence in the context of automation can broadly be classified into the same three groups, just like we saw in *Chapter 2, Robotic Process Automation*.

Take a look at the following diagram to understand the benefits of AI in automation:

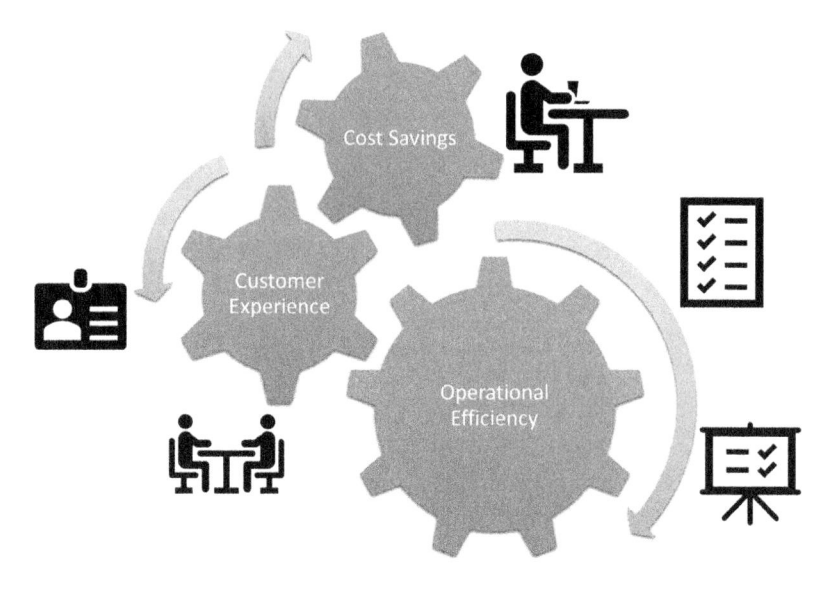

Figure 3.6: Benefits of Artificial Intelligence in Automation

It is important to understand that the benefits derived from Artificial Intelligence in the context of Intelligent Automation are very similar, if not the same, as what we have seen in *Chapter 2, Robotic Process Automation*, as the benefits of RPA. However, since the implementation mechanism is distinctly different for this lever of automations, the RoI achieved may be different across these two levers. To start with, implementing the AI solutions can be often more complex and costly as compared to RPA. A pure AI solution will generate suggestions, recommendations, insights, interpretations and so on, which may not be extremely valuable to an enterprise from the RoI perspective, unless some action is taken based on it. That is where the value of Intelligent Automation comes into play, with AI coming up with the *"best recommended action"* and RPA/microservices *"executing it"*. More importantly, like RPA, the benefits achieved depend greatly on what process is chosen for the AI based automation. It is very important that the right process is chosen and the right kind of data is available for the AI model to train and work. It's only then that the value of this type of automation can be fully achieved.

In the following section, let us understand what makes certain processes better suited for the AI based automation and what are the factors that we should keep in mind when we are selecting the processes/use cases for it.

Fitment of Processes for Artificial Intelligence based Automation

So far, we have discussed about the broad capabilities of AI and the different types of AI that can be leveraged depending upon the problem at hand. Let us now discuss the approach to select the candidate use cases for an AI based automation.

Similar to what we read in *Chapter 2, Robotic Process Automation*, about how the RPA based automation has some key characteristics, the AI based automation also has some key characteristics to gain the maximum value. In most cases, the processes would work on mixed data – structured, unstructured, and semi-structured. There would be a need to analyze and derive decisions in the process which are not completely based on structured rules and have a lot of variations or judgmental decisions. There would be other types of media data processing involved in the process – like voice files, images, video, and so on, that would need processing as part of the automation. As you must have realized by now, each of these criteria is complex and adds to the overall complexity of automation. So, in an Intelligent Automation scenario, where the AI is the brain and RPA are the limbs, obviously the brain has a lot more complex actions to do than the limbs.

Apart from these technical characteristics, there is obviously the non-technical characteristics – like repeatability and labor intensity which adds to the business value that can be derived from the automation.

If we compare some of these characteristics with the ones we discussed for RPA, we will see that there are some straightforward differences. RPA would work best on structured data, whereas AI is needed primarily to analyze, correlate, and interpret unstructured data.

RPA can work with digitized data. Similarly, AI would also need digitized data – that is to say, it would need the image file or the voice file or the video file in a digitized format to work on it. AI would be applicable to process and analyze a much wider and diverse data as compared to RPA.

If we draw a similar representation of the characteristics of the process that makes it suitable for AI – it would be like the following diagram. The process characteristics can broadly be classified into two categories – technical characteristic and non-technical characteristics. Take a look at the following diagram to understand the process fitment criteria for AI based automation:

Technical: (Augmenting Human brain)
Natural language interpretation
Image recognition / processing
Learning and inference
Recommendation
Relevant Data Availability

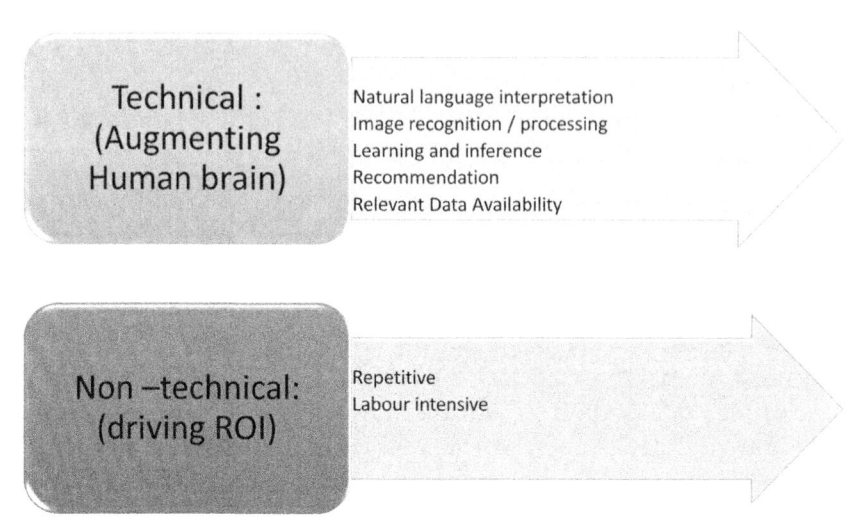

Non –technical: (driving ROI)
Repetitive
Labour intensive

Figure 3.7: Process Fitment Criteria for AI based Automation

Let us now understand in detail, what these characteristics mean, to make it suitable for the automation by AI.

Technical Characteristics of the Process required for AI based Automation

Natural language interpretation: This characteristic means that there is a requirement in the process to communicate with the users in a conversational communication mode without using the technical key words. A very simple example could be when you ask a chatbot – *"How to resolve Order not created"* instead of *"How to resolve ErCoDeOr12X123"*. Siri and Alexa are good examples of Consumer to Business use cases; however, in an enterprise automation scenario, the virtual assistants can be positioned in many domains – starting from assisting the business users using HR, Finance, or Procurement Applications to assisting Support agents/Field agents in resolving tickets.

Image Recognition/Image processing: This is a complex capability of AI and can be very useful in automating a wide range of processes. Identification, interpretation, and analysis of the image – each of these capabilities can be leveraged in the processes to aid automation. From interpreting the data on the image of a form or a document through OCR or Intelligent OCR, extracting the data, to identifying a faulty part from a real time view of an equipment – both could be applicable processes for the image identification and processing capabilities. The possibility is enormous.

Learning and inference: When we think of AI, this is the closest it comes to a human brain – reason, learn, and infer. Sometimes, the human brain does it even without us being aware, like seeing a pothole on the road and avoiding it the next time you cycle on the same road. So, in processes, where there is a requirement to analyze the data and deduce some inference or recognize a pattern and apply that to make additional predictions or recommendation, AI could be a very good fit. Predicting whether a loan applicant would be a defaulter to finding the best car for a customer by a car dealership owner in a locality could all be very apt use cases for the AI based automation.

Recommendation: This is also somewhat related to the preceding characteristic. When there is a requirement for the system to learn, and based on that learning, recommend a set of actions, it would be an AI fit use case. For example, in the IT Operations, based on the analysis of slow order processing events and warnings, there could be a recommendation of purging the logs, releasing some system resources to remediate the events.

Relevant data availability: This is almost a prerequisite to an AI use case. Since the AI solutions are based on analyzing the data and building the models or identifying patterns, based on which the system will respond to future events, a moderate to large volume of data is required to train and test the system for achieving accuracy and performance.

Non-Technical Characteristics of Process required for AI based Automation

These are the same criteria that we discussed in *Chapter 2, Robotic Process Automation*.

The main non-technical characteristics that we need to consider as discussed in the previous chapter is that the process/activity to be automated should generate s significant value or savings, enough to justify the business case for the same. One of the main criteria for the same is that the process should be labor intensive, so that once automated, there can be a reduction of the total effort required to execute the process. However, there can be other factors enabling the savings, like faster time to market, improvement in cycle time, increase in sales/upsell leading to increased revenue generation, better customer experience leading to less churn, and so on, which will also contribute to the value of the automation.

Labor Intensity, as discussed, can be broken down into the following two sub factors:

- Repetitive in nature
- Moderate to high cycle time

The following is a reiteration of the formula, that we learned in *Chapter 2: Robotic Process Automation:*

$$Labor\ Intensity = (frequency * effort)/volume.$$

This may not be the most precise calculation, but in most processes, this will give a fair idea on how to compare and quantify labor intensity.

So, to summarize, the preceding broad characteristics – interaction and interpretation in **Natural language**, **Image processing** and **analysis**, **Learning, Inference and Recommendation** and availability of sufficient data for the preceding, are essential to consider a process fit for the AI based automation. It can, however, be one of the characteristics or a combination, with the data availability being almost a prerequisite.

Based on the preceding assessment criteria, once we have shortlisted the candidate processes, we need to prioritize the processes for automation by AI. For this, we need to consider the same three factors which contribute to the overall return on investment. These are discussed in *Chapter 2:Robotic Process Automation*, and although the factors are the same, the type of assessment may differ from the RPA to AI solutions.

Automatability: This can be defined as the % of steps/tasks in a process that can be automated. Higher the %, the better is the automatability. Usually, this is measured in terms of the total automatability achieved by a combination of multiple technologies like RPA, AI, and others.

Complexity: This would be the level of AI solution complexity of the process to be automated. This is not in direct proportion to the complexity of the process. What this means is that the level of complexity of the AI solution – complexity of the data collation, cleansing, analysis, model build, test, and deploy could be different from the complexity of the process. The process can be moderately complex with several manual judgments involved, but automating those steps could technically be pretty complex.

Benefits: This is a key measure for the prioritization of the use cases. Typically, this is measured in terms of the FTE savings for most automation. However, in the AI based automation, there will most definitely be other benefits like increased accuracy, improved turnaround time, less churn, better customer/employee experience and so on.

The preceding three factors together can give a good indication of which processes should be prioritized for the AI based automation.

Applicability of Artificial Intelligence in Automation through a few typical use cases

Now that we have understood what kind of processes are best fit for the AI are based automation, let us understand a few use cases for them.

In the following sections, we have tried to cover some indicative use cases from different industries and domains. This is a indicative list – not exhaustive at all. These may or may not be completely automated by AI end-to-end, but it would be good to reflect on what makes them a good candidate process for the AI based automation. We will refer to some of these use cases as we discuss Intelligent Automation for Industries in the following chapters.

Financial Services

In most financial institutions, there are systems flagging alerts by the business monitoring systems, monitoring suspicious activities or financial crime. There is a significant number of false positives in these as well. Sieving through this data by the analysts to identify probable cases takes a lot of manual effort and time. There could be an AI based automation to classify these alerts based on the historical data, location, and other parameters to different criticalities (high, medium, low). The low critical ones can be automatically processed, thus letting the investigators focus on the more critical ones.

Know Your Customer (KYC) is another prime area for the AI based automation in the financial services sector. In this process, there are a lot of documents that are usually collected from the customer, and the data needs to be extracted and validated from them. This is a laborious activity and the automated document processing with extraction of relevant entities from the document (image or native doc formats like PDF) and validating them against the standard guidelines would accelerate the time to onboard the customers to the bank. This would lead to significant improvement in the cycle time in completing the KYC process which can sometimes go up to 3-4 weeks.

Customer Behaviour prediction with Customer Churns/Upsell: Managing customer churns and upselling/cross-selling new products and services could also be an interesting use case for the financial institutions where the AI based automation can be leveraged. AI can do the customer profile analysis from the internal and external data, sentiment analysis of the customer, again based on internal and external (e.g., social media) data, and transaction history analysis. Based on such a multi-dimensional analysis, AI can come up with recommendations on the products and services for the customer or predict the churn probability.

Retail

Retail is one of the areas where there is an enormous scope of AI based automation, primarily due to the nature of business and availability of huge volumes of data.

Most of us have used online shopping at some point or another; this usage has accelerated due to the Covid-19 scenario. How many times has it happened that Amazon or Flipkart comes up with the exact product recommendation that you need, or Netflix and Amazon Prime comes up with excellent movie recommendations? In many cases, they relate to our choices and often end up in additional sale for the retailer. Personalized Product and Service Recommendation is one of the leading use cases in Retail for the AI Based automation and is one of the key use cases in this domain.

Optimized Pricing: There may be a use case where a retailer might need to choose the best price from a vendor or supplier. There can be AI models to determine the most optimized price, taking into consideration the various factors like seasons, festival preference, location, and other factors to increase the demand and gain maximum profits.

Customer Behavior Prediction: This could be a similar one like the Financial Services use case, only with different parameters. Based on the analysis of various customers' internal and external data, sentiment analysis, and transaction history, customer behaviors can be predicted, and new services and products can be upsold, or the customer churn prevented.

A similar use case could also be applicable in the telecom industry, where customer behavior is very dynamic. Using the AI based automation to retain the customer and providing them with a better service could increase the revenue as well as the customer base.

Since we are discussing several use cases along similar business process, it would make sense at this point to see what kind of solution might be needed for this type of automation at a high level. To delve a little deeper into this solution, for building a churn model, it could be a classification problem in machine learning. Based on the relevant data like profile, transaction history, social interactions, and so on, we need to predict when in the lifecycle of the customer – provider journey – is the customer most likely to leave. We would need training data, where we need to create such labels in the data, and use this to train the model. This model will be able to provide insights to customer habits who leave and enable the business to take remedial actions to prevent such churn.

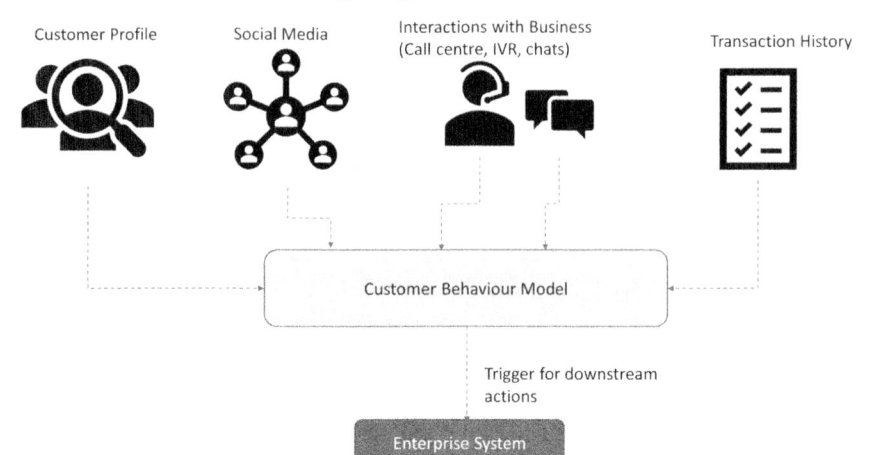

Take a look at the following diagram to understand the churn model:

Figure 3.8: Churn Model

AI in IT Operations Automation

The IT operations is an area in any enterprise which is usually the initial bed for automation. Recently, with Gartner publishing the paper of AIOps, where it advocates leveraging AI in IT Operations, AIOps has become a hot area in this domain.

According to Gartner, AIOps is a platform to enhance the IT Operations with proactive and dynamic insights leveraging big data, machine learning, and other advanced analytics.

This is going to be a prime area for Intelligent Automation, since in most enterprises, there is significant data already available in IT operations – both structured and unstructured – in the form of tickets, logs, alerts, events. A deeper analysis of this data with the help of the machine learning models could bring out big insights to the occurrence of events like downtime, slow performance, high utilization of systems, and others that impact the applications and the other IT infrastructure negatively. With these ready insights, the IT engineers would be able to trigger the downstream remediation with scripts, macros, workflows, or RPA, and achieve the end-to-end automation in the IT operation ecosystem. So, as you can see, this is one area that is going to see a lot of development and traction as we move on. There are already several product and service companies who are packaging AIOps as a service and the list will definitely increase in the coming future. We will discuss AIOps in *Chapter 7: Intelligent Automation – Trends and the Future*.

Other use cases

AI can be applied in a plethora of use cases across the domains and industries. Before we move on to the next topic, the following are a few broad categories where AI can be very aptly applied:

- Fraud detection
- Email processing/spam detection
- Image classification/recognition
- Risk assessment
- Targeted marketing
- Outlier identification

The preceding categories and use cases are again indicative use case categories, and there are many others across all the enterprises. We will discuss some of the use cases in detail and discuss the technical solution in *Chapter 5: Intelligent Automation Usecases*

AI delivery Life cycle

Just like any other technology implementation project, the AI delivery projects also need planning and preparation, and most importantly a clear vision of the AI journey. In the following few sections, we will discuss the various phases of an AI delivery lifecycle.

AI delivery is slightly different in terms of the activities and phases that it includes. Once the problem definition or requirements modeling/user stories are completed, there are two broad activities – building the AI model and refining the model with the current data.

The following section describes the broad phases in a typical AI delivery lifecycle that we discussed earlier in this chapter with Natural Language Processing, Recommendation Engines, and Image Processing. As previously mentioned, the AI projects follow the broad phases as depicted in *figure 3.9* and *figure 3.10*.

The phases can be divided into two broad parts – Phase A – one in which we collect the data, build the data set, and train and refine the model. The second *or* Phase B is testing and refining this model to use with the current live data in hand.

The following diagram depicts Phase A:

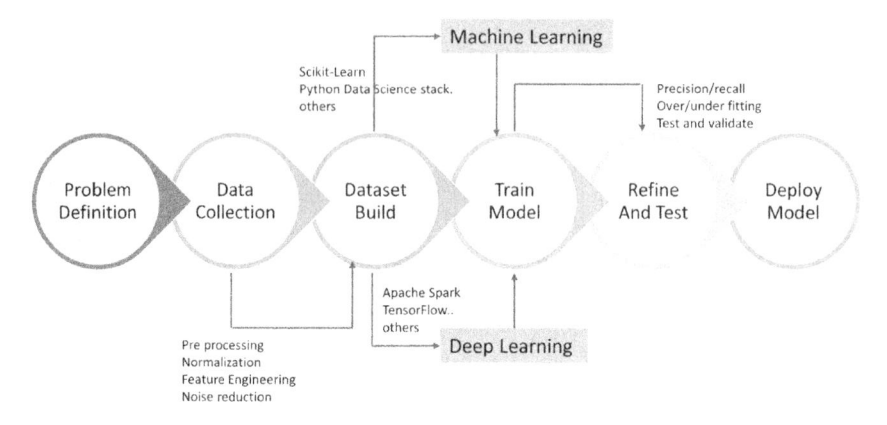

Figure 3.9: *Phase A – Building the model*

The following diagram depicts Phase B:

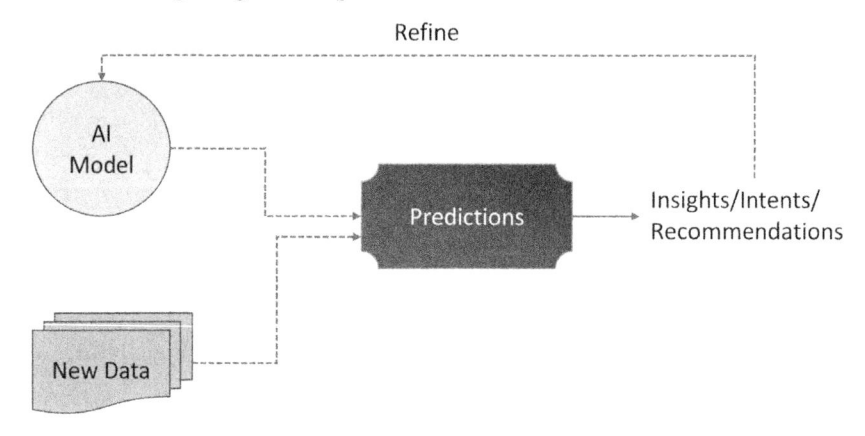

Figure 3.10: *Phase B – Test and refine Model*

Once the model is defined, refined, and deployed, as shown in the preceding diagram, the actual prediction work in the context of the problem in hand is initiated. The current applicable data for the business problem is fed to the model to test the accuracy of the predictions and insights generated. Depending on the results, there may be a need to retrain the model with some modification to the training data set and continue for a few iterations. The duration of this phase might vary, based on the extent of refinement that might need to be done to the model.

Now, let us get into the details of each of these phases.

Use Case Identification and Assessment

The first phase for an AI implementation is identifying the use case and elaborating the problem that we are trying to solve. As discussed earlier, we should select a process/activity for the AI implementation by assessing the technical and non-technical criteria together. This assessment will ensure that not only are we selecting a process that is appropriate for AI implementation from a technical feasibility aspect, but also that the process has significant automation potential and RoI. This becomes very important, once the automation is deployed.

Apart from considering the stakeholder alignment, as in the case of an RPA project, another important consideration for validating the AI use case requirement is the availability of the data. While elaborating the use case, it is essential to identify the data that you would need and how you can make it available. It can be an internally packaged and cleansed data, external data, or a mix or large sets of data which might need a lot of pre-processing. At this stage, it is important to validate that, that data is available and is sufficient since this would impact the feasibility of the implementation of the use case.

Typically, a Business Case is also created during this phase. The idea is to quantify the benefits and calculate the total cost of ownership of the AI automation, which would then be documented in a Business Case and presented for validation to the approving authority.

Data Collection and building Dataset

There is an informative article published in *Forbes* (details in the reference section), which mentions the different stages that the data usually goes through in an AI project. Data is the foundation of the AI system and any model we build will only be as good as the data it builds upon. Hence, it is very important that we put a lot of focus in identifying the data needed, and have a structured method to gather and store this data before moving on to further processing.

Once the data is collected and stored, we need to analyze the data to find out if it is sufficient and if it needs cleansing and any other pre-processing. This is one phase, where most AI projects utilize the maximum effort – preparing and processing the data. Data might need to be normalized and cleansed to reduce noise/aberrations. Feature engineering is an important activity at this stage. Feature engineering is basically extracting the features or parameters from the raw data, based on its domain to leverage it in building and training the AI model and making it contextual to the problem. There is an informative article on feature engineering that I have mentioned in the reference section which you could refer to for a detailed understanding of Feature Engineering. At this stage, we know what the result item is or the entity that needs to be predicted by the AI system. Based on this, the data needs to be appropriately labeled for training as well (in the case of supervised machine learning). At the end of this phase, we should have a training data set as the outcome. This may be the most effort intensive step in the lifecycle, but it is arguably the most important step.

Train the model

Once the dataset is built with cleansed and labeled data, this data is fed to the AI model. The idea is to build a model that can predict the results with precision, based on the data. It is important to use multiple AI models (like decision tree, SVM, random forest etc.) based on the problem statement and decide which one gives the most accurate result. Once an acceptable accuracy is achieved, the model needs to be baselined before moving ahead. This is a very iterative stage and changes should be tracked and managed to produce the best results. There are a few tools in the market that can ingest the data and show you which algorithm can be the best fit. Look up for AutoAI and you would get multiple such tools.

Refine and Test

The next step is to test the model for predictions. There are different strategies to divide the data into test and training sets. Since the AI development details is not in scope of this book, we will not get into those details. But it would be good at this point to take a pause and read up on the different strategies to train and test the model and how you can divide such data sets for both. Based on what strategy you follow, in this step, the AI model should be tested, and the performance needs to be measured. There may be several iterations of refinement of the model, until you reach an acceptable result.

Deploy

Once the model is tested, it is ready to be deployed. It can be deployed on cloud or on-premise, based on the infrastructure requirement and availability. The hardware environment will depend on the non-functional requirements of scalability, availability, volume of data, and the processing power needed to run the model.

Once the model is deployed, in comes the second phase, where you would integrate this solution with the larger ecosystem – where live data will be brought in, and the system will be tested with that. So far, we were working on training and testing the model based on test data. Now, we will test and refine the model with live data. Here, apart from testing the model on the live data set, the data ingestion pipelines may also need to be built and tested. The integration with the data sources, the ETL processes, noise reduction, may need to be automated as a pipeline that will feed the live data into the model to churn out predictions.

As the AI automation goes live, there are several aspects that we need to consider. One is the monitoring part – where just like any other live system, we might need to monitor the system for any failure or errors.

The second aspect is to measure the performance in terms of accuracy. This is an important activity in the whole delivery lifecycle. There are several methods to measure the performance of a model, depending on the type of model you are using. The quantification of the benefits that we did in the business case, need to be mapped with the actual results and any deviation needs to be analyzed and acted upon as feedback loop.

It is important to discuss at this juncture that an AI system may not always deliver the automation benefits completely by itself. The benefit of automation will be achieved, if the insights generated by the AI system are taken forward and executable actions suggested by the AI system are implemented by RPA, Microservices, or the other technologies. This needs to be considered when we are designing the overall automation solution for the system.

Products and tools

This chapter will not be complete if we don't touch upon some of the various AI frameworks and tools available today in the market. In the following table, I have tried to list down a few of the important ones that are prevalent today:

Some common Machine Learning Frameworks

Framework	Website
Scikit-learn	chttps://scikit-learn.org/stable/
Ludwig	https://ludwig-ai.github.io/ludwig-docs/
Stanford CoreNLP	https://stanfordnlp.github.io/CoreNLP/
PyTorch	https://pytorch.org/
Apache SparkMLlib	https://spark.apache.org/mllib/
Amazon Machine Learning	https://aws.amazon.com/machine-learning/
Azure ML Studio	https://azure.microsoft.com/en-in/services/machine-learning/
Watson Machine Learning	https://www.ibm.com/in-en/cloud/machine-learning

Table 3.1: Common Machine Learning Frameworks

Some common Deep Learning Frameworks

Framework	Website
TensorFlow	https://www.tensorflow.org/
Keras	https://keras.io
Caffe	https://caffe.berkeleyvision.org/
ONNX	https://onnx.ai/
PyTorch	https://pytorch.org/
DeepLearning4J	https://deeplearning4j.org/
Microsoft Cognitive Toolkit	https://docs.microsoft.com/en-us/cognitive-toolkit/
Theano	https://pypi.org/project/Theano/

Table 3.2: Common Deep Learning Frameworks

This is not an exhaustive list, and there are many others that are prevalent with similar capabilities.

As you can see, AI is gaining more momentum as a key lever in the overall Intelligent Automation space. There are many products and frameworks available and you might need to evaluate these to determine the framework of choice based on the enterprise's requirements.

Another important point that I want to touch upon here is that in today's organizations with complex processes and business models, there may not be a single tool or framework that can be applied across the whole enterprise. With varied requirements, skills, and infrastructure available, a combination of open source frameworks along with off the shelf vendor frameworks may be needed to be evaluated to create the optimum AI framework.

Conclusion

In this chapter, we understood what AI based automation is and how it contributes as a key component in the automation landscape. We also discussed the various characteristics of AI based automation, what kind of processes should be automated with AI, and the broad benefits that can be achieved. We then discussed what the maximum benefit from the AI based automation is when such automation works in combination with the downstream systems triggering actions based on the insights generated by AI.

We also discussed the AI delivery method and understood the different phases and the important considerations in each phase. Lastly, we touched upon a snapshot of some of the AI tools and frameworks available in the market. I would like to leave you with this thought in mind that AI is a very powerful and integral component of Intelligent Automation now. It is what makes the automation intelligent and is the way forward as the enterprises mature in their automation journey.

In the next chapter, we will discuss about a few more technologies like the blockchain and the Internet of Things, which also play a part in achieving Intelligent Automation in the enterprise.

References

1. Shaping the Future of Technology Governance: Artificial Intelligence and Machine Learning - **https://www.weforum.org/platforms/shaping-the-future-of-technology-governance-artificial-intelligence-and-machine-learning**

2. The Fourth Industrial Revolution: what it means, how to respond -**https://www.weforum.org/agenda/2016/01/the-fourth-industrial-revolution-what-it-means-and-how-to-respond/**

3. Alan Turing - **https://www.britannica.com/biography/Alan-Turing**

4. Alan Turing article - **http://www.alanturing.net/turing_archive/pages/Reference%20Articles/What%20is%20AI.html**

5. Types of Machine Learning - **https://blogs.oracle.com/datascience/types-of-machine-learning-and-top-10-algorithms-everyone-should-know-v2** ; **https://www.ibm.com/in-en/analytics/machine-learning**

6. **AIOps Platform - https://blogs.gartner.com/andrew-lerner/2017/08/09/aiops-platforms/**

7. Forbes: Data is the Foundation of AI - **https://www.forbes.com/sites/willemsundbladeurope/2018/10/18/data-is-the-foundation-for-artificial-intelligence-and-machine-learning/?sh=b3048be51b49**

8. Feature Engineering - **https://towardsdatascience.com/feature-engineering-for-machine-learning-3a5e293a5114**

9. Evaluation of ML Algorithm - **https://towardsdatascience.com/metrics-to-evaluate-your-machine-learning-algorithm-f10ba6e38234**

Chapter 4
Other Technologies in Automation

Introduction

In *Chapter 1, Intelligent Automation*, we discussed that in Intelligent Automation, several technologies come together to enable an end-to-end automation of a process. It is, in essence, a convergence of technologies to achieve the end-to-end automation in a business or IT process. We also discussed the two foundational pillars of Intelligent Automation's Robotic Process Automation and Artificial Intelligence. However, there are other technology levers which bring in their unique capabilities, like BPM or Integration. These are matured and have been prevalent for a long time but are still demonstrating their value in forming the base of an Intelligent Automation paradigm. The blockchain and Internet of Things or IoT, are new and yet to be adopted on a wider scale.

In this chapter, we will talk about the blockchain and Internet of Things, which can have an important contribution to the Intelligent Automation ecosystem. These technologies have not yet picked up in a big way like RPA and AI, but they have significant potential to cause a deep impact. With the advent of 5G in the next few years, IoT is going to have a major impact in automation. In this chapter, we will discuss them as the technology enablers of Intelligent Automation, how they impact and transform automation, the benefits they can bring, and how to plan an automation journey with these technologies in an enterprise.

We will also touch upon Workflow and Integration briefly to appreciate their importance. Let us now get started with an overview of these technologies, a few use cases, and any special consideration that needs to be kept in mind while designing an Intelligent Automation system with all these technologies brought together.

Structure

In this chapter, we will cover the following topics:

- Other technologies – Blockchain, IoT, Workflow, and Integration
- Brief overview on each of these technologies
- Best suited use cases
- Best practices

Objective

After reading this chapter, you will be able to understand the necessity of the blockchain, IoT, Workflow, and Integration in Intelligent Automation and their applicability in automation through the various use cases and scenarios that we will discuss as we progress in the chapter. You will also be able to understand and articulate the benefits that these technologies can bring and imbibe a few best practices that will be handy while you design and develop the solutions around these technologies in the context of Intelligent Automation.

Blockchain

In this section, let us get an overview of the blockchain technology, its key characteristics, and how it works. The blockchain can be viewed as a distributed and decentralized ledger technology that is used to maintain the history of an asset and record the transactions. An asset can be anything like a car, an object, or cash, or it could be anything intangible as well, like IP (intellectual property). Being shared and immutable makes it trustworthy and it preserves the integrity of all the ledger changes. A blockchain promises to bring a lot of transparency in transactions along with a reduction in risks and frauds. The concept of nodes in the blockchain technology makes it decentralized. No single entity can own the chain. The distributed ledger is distributed via the nodes, each node maintaining a copy of the chain. A blockchain network is ideal to deliver the information to all the interested parties in a trusted and transparent manner since the distributed ledger is immutable and can be updated only by the network members with adequate permissions. This results in having a single source of truth and all the members of the chain can see the single version at any point in time.

The blockchain networks can be public, private, or permissioned. A public blockchain does not need any permission for a party to join or update the network. A private blockchain is one which can be joined only by invitation. It is a closed network within an organization and has strong access and authorization mechanisms. There are controls in place to allow the parties to join or transact in the chain network.

A permissioned blockchain lies in between the public and private chains in terms accessibility and permissions. It has an access control layer that enables actions to be performed by only certain entities with relevant permissions.

One of the key and popular features of blockchain is **smart contracts**. A smart contract is a self-enforcing agreement between the parties in the chain that is executed based on certain predefined conditions. It is usually a set of transactions that are executed as part of the smart contract and sent to the other parties in the network automatically. Smart contract in a blockchain has found interesting use cases in various industries and domains like the supply chain, insurance, and others. Smart contracts are an interesting capability of the blockchain that makes it very suited to be an important technological element in the Intelligent Automation ecosystem.

In this chapter, we will not dive deep into the blockchain as a technology but will cover it more from an Intelligent Automation perspective. I have added a few references which can give you more details around some of these topics.

Take a look at the following diagram to understand the characteristics of a blockchain:

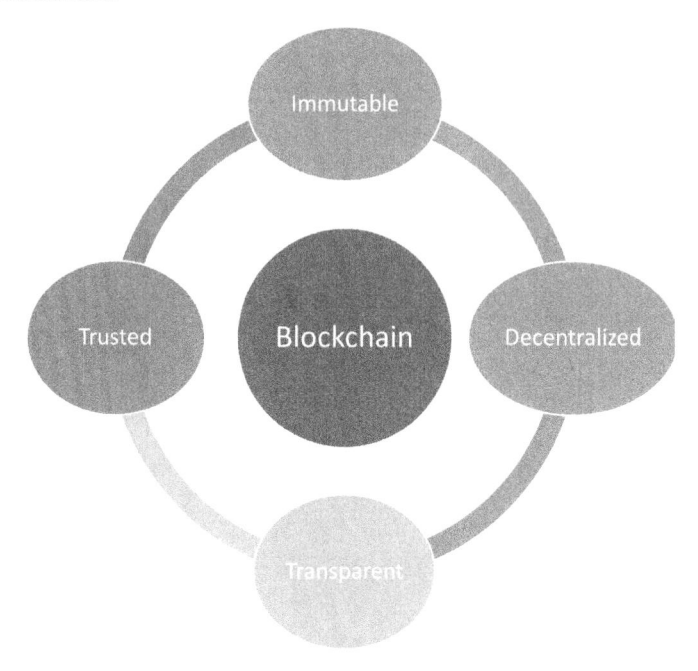

Figure 4.1: *Characteristics of Blockchain*

With this overview of the blockchain that we discussed earlier, let us now try to understand how a blockchain acts as a contributing technology in Intelligent Automation.

Think of the characteristics of a blockchain and how they can add value to the common use cases like record keeping, logistics management, tracking goods, and so on. Each of these scenarios need immutability to prevent the tampering of unwanted interference, and they need auditability and traceability and one single source of accurate data.

The popular use cases of blockchain, thus include record management, asset tracking and management, legal ownership management, and so on. In the following sections, we will dive deeper into a few of these use cases and try to see how a blockchain contributes to automating these use cases.

The adoption of blockchain in the industries has been slow but some of the industries have become the early adopters and moving towards maturity. Financial Services is one of the early adopters. Since a blockchain promises to reduce the risk of fraud and unwanted tampering of the data, there is a natural alignment of the Financial Services industry to leverage the blockchain technology. A leading bank, Banco Santander has leveraged the blockchain technology for automating the cross-border money transfer securely(see reference).. The immutability and transparency in the transactions in a blockchain has made it fit to be positioned in such use cases.

The blockchain implementation leveraging the smart contract capability is also gaining momentum in building Intelligent Automation. A leading insurance provider Axa, has implemented a product in travel insurance, using the smart contract technology to automatically initiate the pay outs to the customers based on the delay in flights(see reference).

As you can see, a blockchain can be effectively leveraged across the industries; however, the key is to identify the best fit use cases. Just like for RPA and AI, there are a few key characteristics that make a use case fit for the blockchain implementation. Let us understand that in the following section.

Fitment of processes for blockchain based automation

So far, we have discussed about the broad capabilities of the blockchain as a technology and seen a few examples where it has been implemented to address a varied set of business problems. Let us now discuss the approach to select the candidate use cases for Intelligent Automation that can leverage the blockchain.

The following are some of the key criteria of the process or the sub-process that make it suitable for the blockchain implementation:

Immutability

The transactions in the process or sub process need to be immutable and cannot be changed after it has been recorded in the ledger. No party should be able to overwrite such a transaction and in case of an error, a new transaction needs to be recorded to reverse the error.

Single source of truth

The process to be automated through the blockchain should have a requirement to provide for a single source of truth for an entity – it could be the state of a claim, the ownership of an IP, and so on. The requirement is that, there should be one single authentic view of the record.

Traceable provenance

Another requirement of the process to be automated by the blockchain is that there is a need to track and record the entity or the asset right from where it originated to its final state. All the transactions which have been executed on that should be recorded and traceable.

Trust

This is one of the key requirements for a process to be implemented with the blockchain as one of the levers of automation. There should be a need to ensure that the parties involved in the transactions trust each other based on a consensus between them.

As you can very well identify, these are also the key characteristics of the blockchain as a technology. So, wherever there are such requirements from the automation of a process to bring in these capabilities, the blockchain can be considered and assessed for fitment.

A key point to be noted is that some of the requirements mentioned here may be fulfilled by implementing the strict data integrity rules in data management. There can be other ways of fulfilling these requirements as well. So, while evaluating the technology lever, we need to view it holistically. There needs to be a conscious and well-thought out technical and business justification for why the blockchain may be required to implement the use case. In many cases, the final points that we discussed on *'Trust'* and *'Immutability'* may act as the deciding factors on whether to implement a blockchain or not.

Just as what we saw in *Chapter 2* on Robotic Process Automation and *Chapter 3* on AI, the fitment of a technology depends on the technical as well as the non-technical criteria. The technical criteria was discussed earlier in this chapter. Apart from these technical criteria, the non-technical criteria should also be assessed for the fitment of a blockchain. That non-technical criterion remains the same for most of the automation levers, since it is geared towards achieving the business value of automation through cost savings, increase in efficiency, and accuracy and improvement in customer experience. Hence, the factors like repeatability, labor intensiveness, and adherence to SLA of the process should be considered while assessing the business criteria of the process fitment.

The following figure summarizes the technical and non-technical characteristics of a process that should be assessed to find out the fitment of a blockchain as a lever to implement Intelligent Automation:

Technical : Immutability, Trust, Traceable Provenance, Single Source of Truth

Non –technical: (driving ROI) Repetitive, Labour intensive

Figure 4.2: Factors to assess the fitment of Blockchain in Intelligent Automation

Blockchain use cases for Intelligent Automation

By now, you have got an understanding of what a blockchain can do and what kind of processes would be a good fit for automation by the blockchain. Let us now discuss a few use cases that are relevant and applicable for Intelligent Automation with a blockchain.

Digital identity and inheritances

Digital Identity refers to those digital entities which help establish our identity and are usually issued by the governments or equivalent institutions; for example, the Passport or Aadhar Card in India.

Digital identity

You must have heard of and used DigiLockers. In DigiLockers, only the authentic owner of the locker or ID issuer can add or edit the documents in the locker and the other eligible parties should be able to view it. A blockchain can be used for managing the Digital Identification. Personal digital ids like Passport, Driving License, and so on, that are issued by the Government agencies can be stored and managed by the owners of the identities. Only select parties will have the permission to modify them while most parties will be able to leverage them for the identification and authentication purposes. A blockchain based digital identity can provide an interoperable, secure, and tamperproof entity that would provide value to both the individuals and the enterprises. Digital lockers can use the blockchain technology to ensure that the owners of the lockers are in control and aware of any entity using or attempting to tamper with their information.

Inheritances and Wills

An interesting use case could be around the way the wills and inheritances are created and processed. As per legal requirements, wills should be immutable and not be tampered or modified by anyone other than the individual who created the will. How can this be enforced digitally? The individuals can create digital wills with a blockchain technology embedded to prevent any tampering of the will. The individual can distribute the will among their inheritances, and based on smart contract, it can automatically be executed when the individual dies. Think of the implication of automating this use case for the Legal Service Provider firm. They will be able to save significant time and money and deploy their super skilled team of lawyers for more complex cases.

Financial services

As discussed in the preceding section, the blockchain technology-based automation has a strong affinity towards being leveraged in the financial services sector based on the property of immutability and provenance. A few such scenarios are listed in the following section.

Capital markets

Capital Markets can radically transform with a blockchain. Though at a nascent stage, a blockchain shows enough promise to be leveraged in the asset management, issuance and offerings of securities, sales and trading, and even in the post-trade services and custody management. Inherently immutable at the core, a blockchain reduces the risk of fraud, increases efficiency, and reduces the cycle time.

Financial record keeping

The inherent characteristics of a blockchain also make it suitable for implementing the automation in record keeping, especially the financial record keeping. Since the owners of the chain can control the amount of information that can be shared and modified while maintaining trust, and also provide a single snapshot of the data, record keeping can drastically transform if a blockchain is adopted at scale.

Logistics

The blockchain has wide usage in the logistics industry. The Shipping and Logistics companies are suffering losses due to inefficient practices around theft, middleman, and brokers, and spoilage of the perishables. Stolen cargo and misplaced goods are some of the key pain points of a logistics company. A blockchain based distributed ledger to track and monitor the goods at every point and avoid any unnecessary and unwarranted interference with the goods, will not only make the operations more efficient but also reduce the theft and misplacement of the goods. An automation of such logistics operation process with the blockchain could very well have a justifiable business case with the high RoI numbers.

The preceding use cases are just a few examples, and they give a glimpse of a few scenarios where the blockchain can be used to build Intelligent Automation. Though the blockchain has showed significant promise, it is yet to be adopted at scale for commercial purposes. There are higher adoptions across some industries, which is happening in pockets due to various reasons. These reasons range from the lack of appropriate fitment of use cases to higher cost and deployment of the implemented projects and unjustified RoI, thus creating the technical and the business constraints in large scale adoption.

To sum up, in the context of Intelligent Automation, a blockchain can be considered as one of the levers depending on the nature and character of the process under consideration. But one needs to weigh the pros and cons carefully during such fitment with focus on the technical feasibility and commercial viability.

Let us now look at another powerful technology, Internet of Things that has a huge promise, and with the advent of 5G in the near future, it can radically transform our lives and society with Intelligent Automation.

Internet of Things

Internet of Things (IoT) can be explained as a network of *"things"*, which include sensors, devices, software, and so on, that can communicate over a network and exchange the data for various purposes. The sensors and devices collect the data from the environment that they are embedded in. This data can be used in many ways – to arrive at decisions, to predict the next best actions, to execute the next fit transactions, and so on among other things. The availability of continuous data makes it possible for decisions to be recommended and actions to be predicted automatically by the system, which otherwise might have needed human analysis. This makes IoT a key enabler for the data driven decisioning, thus enabling Intelligent Automation.

So how does IoT work?

In the Internet of Things environment, there are multiple devices connected to a network and each have a unique identifier. These devices have the capability to sense and gather data about the environment in which they are embedded. This data is then transferred to a central system, where the data can be collated, analyzed, and used for further processing. It is this data that enables IoT to be an important lever in the whole Intelligent Automation ecosystem. A continuous stream of data provides an immense opportunity to generate insights by leveraging AI or analytics, which could be used to automate a business process. In fact, such data driven decision making in a process is what makes it a smart process. Hence, the importance of IoT in Intelligent Automation is significant.

Internet of Things has been prevalent for a while, with some industries taking the lead in its adoption. The RFID tags are used commonly to track items in manufacturing and logistics for quite some time. In today's time, almost every car is mandated to have the RFID tags for the toll payment on the National Highways in India. With the passage through a toll gate, the RFID tag is read and the account associated with the tag is debited with the relevant sum of money. That's Internet of Things in live action that automates the toll payment and lays down the foundation of an intelligent transportation system in India.

Characteristics of IoT

The characteristics of IoT is broadly described in the following diagram:

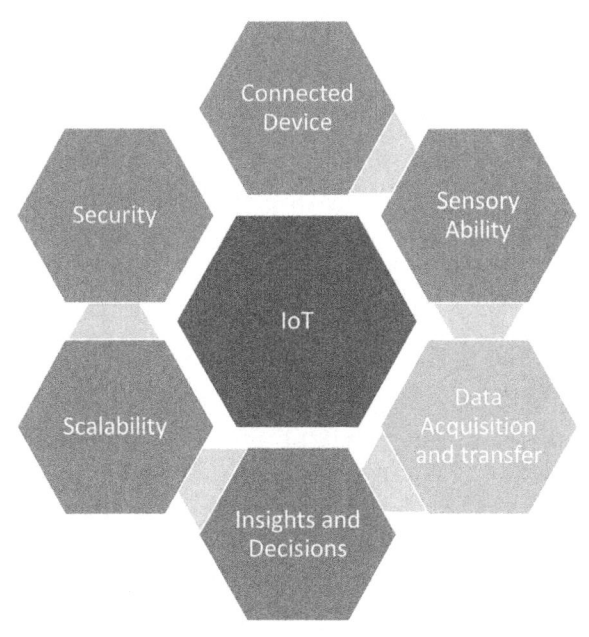

Figure 4.3: Characteristics of Internet of Things

Connected devices

The devices are the *"things"* in IoT. These could be a heterogeneous set of devices that can connect over a network. The communication protocols can vary – it could be over the radio waves, Wi-Fi, Bluetooth, and others. The devices can have elective features like energy efficiency, low power utilization, automatic start and switch off, and so on, to make them more adaptable to the environment they will operate in.

Sensing ability

This is the key characteristic of IoT. The connected devices should be able to sense any change in the environment that they are embedded in. The sensors can monitor, track, and measure the device activities and interactions with the environment.

Data acquisition and transfer

Powered with the sensory abilities, the connected devices should have the processing power to gather the data from the environment and transmit them to the central systems for processing.

Data processing

This is the heart of the IoT system. This is where the data that is transmitted by the devices is processed to generate insights using AI and Analytics. The data processing needs to be fast and efficient – it could be typically hosted on cloud for the obvious scalability benefits.

Scalability

This is an important characteristic of IoT. The devices and their connectivity over networks using the different protocols and the processing unit that gathers the data and applies algorithms to derive insights or recommend actions – all these entities of the IoT ecosystem need to scale for an efficient and effective IoT system.

Security

Security is an essential characteristic and needs to be managed at multiple levels. One of the levels is the physical security of the embedded devices to prevent vandalism and tampering. The other level is the security of the data – during acquisition, transfer, and storage. This, thus, encompasses network security, data security, as well as application security to enable a secured IoT ecosystem. However, the level of security might vary on a scenario or use case basis.

IoT Use cases

Smart Homes and Smart Cities are some of the most common IoT based Intelligent Automation scenarios. Motion sensing lights are now very common and a household phenomenon – the wearables tracking and measuring different health parameters are using that to make predictions, and it is becoming common; the refrigerators fitted with IoT and integrated with the online retail portal are beginning their foray into our lives. Connected Cars is another example of IoT based automation. That's the tag line of one the leading car manufacturers in India and they provide the IoT based automation for predicting faults and issues with the car and providing service reminders to the car owners. In each of these examples, the principle is the same. There are a host of IoT devices, sensing any change in the object they are sembedded in. The data is collected from the IoT devices and the AI models are applied on this data to generate insights. These are acted upon to positively impact the outcome of the process in a faster and more accurate manner, thus resulting in the automation of the process.

If you take a closer look at what we just discussed, you will see that the automation leverages several technologies in these use cases. There is a clear convergence of technologies – IoT, AI, Integration – all are in play, and such aggregated synchronization results in the automation of a process.

Let us discuss a few more use cases and how Intelligent Automation can be achieved by IoT in their context.

The industrial sector deals with large machines, their manufacturing, sales, and services. With IoT, these machines could be equipped with sensors to provide real time data on the health of the machinery. This data could be analyzed not only to assess the current health of the machine but also predict which part has a higher probability of breaking down. With this insight generated, there could a chain of events and actions triggered to initiate a proactive service of the machine, thus preventing downtime and eventual customer delight. Industrial IoT or IIoT is also gaining a lot of momentum. Along with AI and analytics, the IIoT enabled Intelligent Automation promises to bring improvement in reliability and efficiency of the operations in the industrial sector.

The whole concept of smart cities is based on Intelligent Automation primarily driven by IoT. Surveillance through CCTV, Street Lighting, Traffic Management – each of these aspects include sensory devices in the respective environments. The data transmitted by the devices is used to generate actionable insights. These insights are then acted upon by downstream systems to automate the end-to-end process.

The IoT based Intelligent Automation use cases are spread across the industry. It's applicable in healthcare – with wearables and digital health trackers, fall prevention mechanisms, remote patient tracking – all of which are based on sensory devices sending out the data to the data processing platforms. These generate actionable insights which can then be executed by the downstream system. For example, in the fall prevention use cases, if the sensory device detects a fall, It could call 911, or dial an ambulance, or dial the next of kin based on the impact it has sensed. The possibilities are enormous.

Retail could be completely transformed with the IoT based Intelligent Automation. The sensors attached to the products could automate the whole supply chain – it can track the movement of a product and predict its accurate time of arrival. It can also provide valuable data to relate the position of a product in a shelf to its sale. This data could be used to build the AI models to recommend product positioning on a shelf which could eventually boost the sales.

Smart Logistics, Connected Cars, Smart Meters, Smart building – all point to the IoT based automation and the possibilities are endless.

One key point about the IoT based Intelligent Automation is that this cannot be complete without the support of a strong and fast network and the applicability of AI or Analytics to derive value from the IoT data. In itself, the data transmitted and collected cannot benefit automation. It is on the basis of the data and the algorithms generating the decisions from this data that makes the automation possible. In the traditional scenario, there would be humans working for hours on a fraction of the volume of data to make the predictions and create actionable insights. That is the value of automation in such a case.

What makes a process fit for the IoT implementation in Intelligent Automation?

Fitment of processes for the IoT based Automation

Like the other technology levers, in case of IoT too, the business case needs to be justified. The non-technical characteristics of the process to justify the business case remains almost the same – the value derived based on the savings of the labor and the nontangible benefit by the improvement of the customer or employee experience.

The following is a graphical representation of the technical and non-technical characteristics of a process that makes it suitable for automation by IoT:

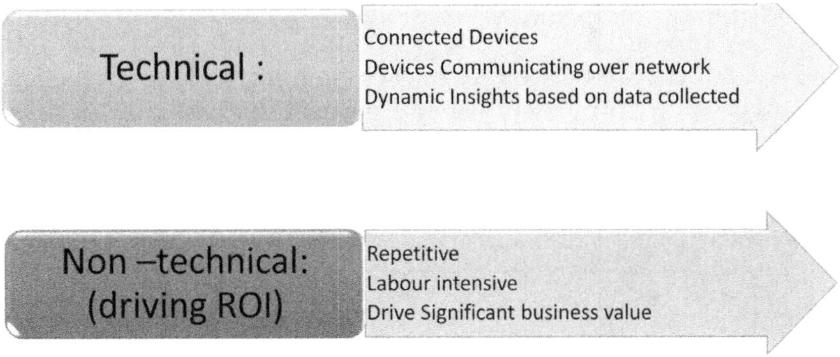

Technical :
- Connected Devices
- Devices Communicating over network
- Dynamic Insights based on data collected

Non –technical: (driving ROI)
- Repetitive
- Labour intensive
- Drive Significant business value

Figure 4.4: *What makes a process fit for IoT based Intelligent Automation*

The non-technical characteristics of the process, as you might have realized by now, is as important as the technical characteristics to justify the business case. The process selected for automation should be able to bring business value. It could be in terms of labor savings or improvement in the customer and employee experience.

Delivering IoT Projects

Now let us quickly touch upon some of the important considerations to keep in mind while delivering the IoT based Intelligent Automation.

The IoT based automation projects could encompass a lot of unknown territory since a significant part of it is based on devices. An evaluation of the devices depending on the requirements may be needed to identify whether the sensory capabilities and interface interoperability meets the desired requirements. Typically, there may be vendors or partners working together – one working on the device hardware and services associated with the device and the other on the server-side data collation, analysis, and inferences. A tight integration between the two is essential, and hence the management of such a project is key to the success. I have seen IoT projects starting with a short Proof of Concept or a Pilot with minimum requirements preceding a production implementation. This approach helps to mitigate the risk of the unknowns that may arise because of the various hardware and software integration and compatibility issues. Also important is the network connectivity and bandwidth for the connectivity between the devices and the software, as well as for the speed of the data transmission.

The following diagram, *figure 4.5* depicts a typical journey to a Proof of Concept or Pilot; post a successful delivery of the PoC or Pilot, the following agile method of delivery, iteratively MVPs or minimum viable products can be built, with each iteration picking on the key use cases and building on top of one another:

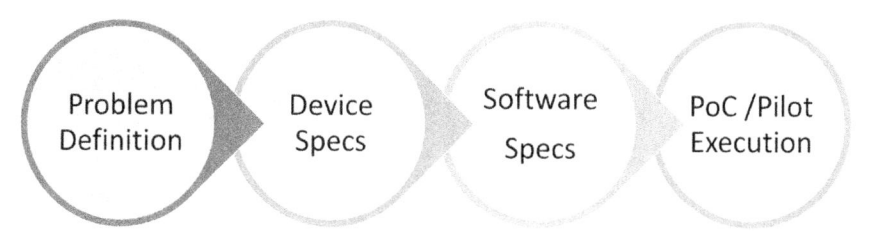

Problem Definition → Device Specs → Software Specs → PoC/Pilot Execution

Figure 4.5: Approach for an IoT MVP or PoC

By now, you have got a fairly good idea of how IoT can be leveraged in Intelligent Automation. There is an excellent report by the World Economic Forum (WEF) which stresses on how the Internet of Things are changing the way things work around us – how it is making the world smarter. It's a good read in this context; you can find it in the References section.

Before we proceed to the other technologies, let us pause and see where we are. At this point, let me bring up the figure that we discussed in *Chapter 1, Introduction to Intelligent Automation*; take a look at the following diagram, which shows the technological convergence in Intelligent Automation:

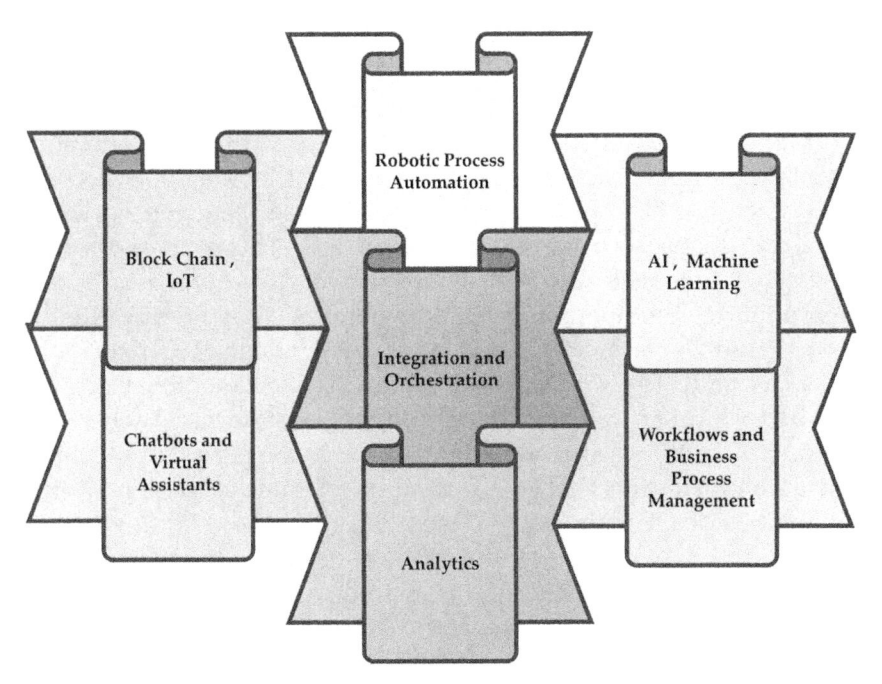

Figure 4.6: Technological Convergence in Intelligent Automation

By now, you must have perceived and are convinced that to achieve Intelligent Automation, there may not be one single technology lever. We have discussed RPA in *Chapter 2*, AI and Chatbots in *Chapter 3*, and Blockchain and IoT in this chapter. You are probably appreciating the jigsaw puzzle type look of the preceding diagram and the concept of the pieces fitting together to create the whole picture of Intelligent Automation.

Let us now move towards two more topics – Workflow and Integrations. These might sound common place and not as glamorous a technology as the ones we discussed earlier, like the blockchain and IoT. These have also been prevalent for a long time – and they remain as the important pillars in the Intelligent Automation ecosystem.

Workflow

A workflow is a series of tasks that are executed in a definite sequence to complete a process or sub-process. A workflow usually has an input, an output, business rules, and several data entities that are usually transformed, created, and deleted during the execution of the workflow.

Workflows are core to any business or IT operations. Workflows can help automate repeatable processes and activities which follow a defined sequence and are guided by the business rules. Typically, the workflows are executed repeatedly to achieve a business outcome. There are steps and activities in the sequence that are dependent on each other. For example, there could be a Case Manager workflow to create, manage, track, and close a case. These are extremely repeatable processes and not having a workflow could be a real pain point for the operations teams where they have to execute the tasks manually and also manage the dependencies between the tasks manually. The workflows streamline such sequential execution and allow human intervention through user interfaces whenever required. Workflows also allow integration to the peripheral systems and automated data fetching or updating based on the integration capabilities of the interfacing systems. Hence, the workflows have become the foundation of automation in any enterprise. Most matured enterprises already have well-developed workflows and, in many cases, start their Intelligent Automation journey with this foundation. However, there are many enterprises which may not be as matured in terms of the IT enablement of business processes. In such scenarios, it would be prudent to identify the processes which could be automated by the workflows.

Fitment of processes for Workflow based Automation

The characteristics of a process that makes it fit for a workflow implementation are, in a way, like what we have seen for RPA. The key questions to ask could be around the following topics:

- Is there is a well-defined process with a sequence of activities that need to be executed in order?
- Are they based on rules?
- What kind of decision points are there in the process?
- What are the interfacing systems and are they API enabled?
- Is there variability in the process and how are the variations defined (by rules)?

These questions, as you can see, are pretty similar to the factors that we considered for deciding whether RPA would be a technology lever. One of the deciding factors in the debate between a bot or a workflow is the integration mechanism with peripheral systems. If APIs are available, then having an automated workflow becomes feasible and much more efficient for the execution of the process right away. In case all peripheral systems are not exposing APIs, then in order to have an automated process, there may be additional automation needed – it could be an RPA bot for the activity on a system that is not API enabled or executed on the proprietary legacy system. However, there could be other strategic mechanisms like exposing it as a microservice with modernization efforts on the respective application. What is important here is, like all technical decisions, whether to automate using a workflow or a combination of other levers, this one should be driven by the best fit technology and optimum cost.

The market for the workflow software and more advanced Business Process Management is matured and is stable with several off-the-shelf products that can be leveraged. Most of these come with a content manager to store and manage the documents associated with the workflow, a process designer that makes it easy to design and configure the workflow, and a rules engine to serve as a central repository of rules.

In the context of Intelligent Automation, this is significant. If you have noticed, the characteristics of a workflow are remarkably similar to the characteristics of a process that is for the RPA based automation. What that means is that the same process can be automated by RPA as well. However, automating many processes in an enterprise with RPA may not be the best solution if the same can be done with workflows. Typically, workflows are more efficient, flexible, and configurable than the RPA bots, not to mention, the cost of ownership and maintenance in the long run.

In a workflow, apart from the input, output, and transformation, there are interfaces with the other enterprise systems where the data entities are created or modified. If the systems interacting with the workflow expose APIs, then the workflow might be the best solution for automating the whole process. In case they are not, and if manual integration or manual operation is needed, then the automation solution might include the workflow, plus an RPA bot for a specific task or activity. Say, within the workflow, there is a system from where data needs to be read and matched, and the application does not have an API. In such a case, a bot working on top of the workflow may be a good solution.

So, the key point is that the nature of the process characteristics for the fitment of a workflow and RPA may be similar, but RPA should be used when we have analyzed and assessed that the workflow may not be a fit – both from the technical and the non-technical perspectives. For example, if the process is a tactical one, with a short lifespan (less than a year before planned decommissioning), then it could make sense to implement a tactical bot, before deciding on the strategic solution of a workflow, which in this case, could be more expensive, if not an overkill.

As is the case with all the architectures and solutions, the fitment of the various technological solutions is contextual and based on specific requirements – functional, non-functional, and of course the constraints of the ecosystem. While identifying the use cases and deciding on the technical solutions, all these factors need to be considered and assessed to derive at the optimum solution, both from conformance to requirements and viability of ownership.

Integration

Integration is an especially important glue that connects the different systems. In Intelligent Automation, it is the key ingredient that is making the end-to-end automation possible. So far, all the technologies that we have discussed as the lever for Intelligent Automation are kind of focused on a set of specific requirements. For example, AI will automate decisioning, RPA will automate manual activities, and Workflows will automate the activities in a sequence. But what holds them together is the integration between them all. As readers of this book, I am sure you understand and realize the importance of integration and its different patterns in the software application ecosystem. I will not dive deep into integration since that is not only a huge area, but also because, most of us with some background on delivering software projects already have some knowledge about the different integration patterns and techniques. The following is a link for an easy reference with a lot of good articles and free books: **https://www.enterpriseintegrationpatterns.com/**.

Now that we have discussed all the technological pieces that make up Intelligent Automation, it is important to reflect how it all comes together. As technologists and evangelists, we tend to get carried away by the technologies and their immense possibilities. But we need to keep in mind that technology is not the driver – it is the enabler for the automation. What is driving Intelligent Automation is the business benefits associated with the automation – in terms of cost savings, customer and employee experience, and an overall improvement in operational efficiency. This point is particularly important since I have seen that, sometimes, it is easy to get entangled in the plethora of technical decisions and lose focus on the key business problem that we are trying to solve.

Use cases

Let us now go through a very common process in the supply chain. Think of the grains, fruits, vegetables, and so on, that we need to consume in our day-to-day lives. The process from produce to consume can very simplistically be described via *figure 4.7*.

The farmer produces his grains, vegetables, and fruits and sells it to a broker or middleman who is usually local. The broker then sells it to the wholesaler and arranges the shipment to the wholesaler. The wholesaler has different distributors associated with him and delivers defined amounts of the produce to the distribution centers. The retail stores then procure this from the distribution centers and finally put it up for sale for the consumers.

Take a look at the following diagram to understand the producer-consumer cycle:

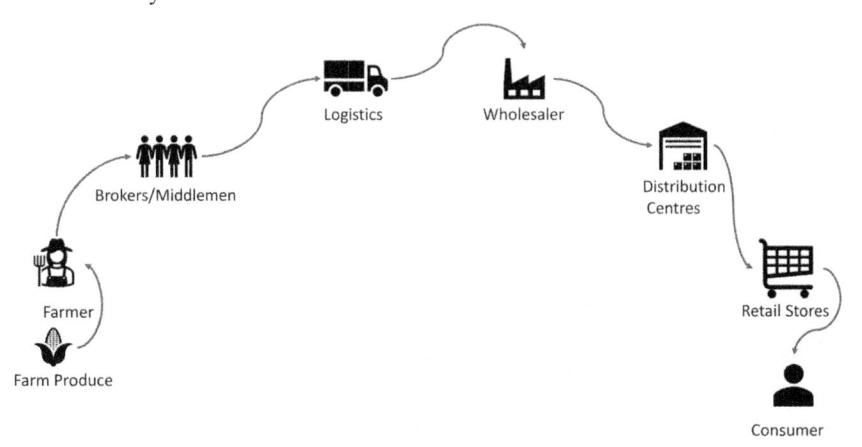

Figure 4.7: From Farm to the Store – Producer-Consumer Cycle

The process, as you can see in the preceding diagram, is complex. There is a high risk of unwanted interference at each step that might cause a loss in quality and price. The process is highly repeatable and is executed at high frequency. There is a lot of manual activity, tracking, monitoring, and decisioning involved to ensure the successful completion of the process. Let us now think how we can automate this process with all that we have learnt so far.

Realistically speaking, parts of the process in most scenarios will already be partly automated, especially for the large wholesalers and distributers supplying to the large retail chains. However, there is still a lot of potential for automation. The benefits can be identified as labor savings, quicker time to market, and greater operational efficiency, among others. Quantifying these in a specific context of a use case will help us arrive at a good business case.

Now let us think of how the Intelligent Automation levers can be applied to automating the process. An immutable audit trail achieved by the blockchain could ensure that the produce that was sold by the farmer reaches the consumer in an acceptable state, without being adulterated. An IoT based automation in the cycle from the wholesaler to the retail stores can ensure that the right quantity of produce reaches the right stores at the right time. An AI based model, predicting the volume of produce and the demand of produce depending on the season, locale etc., can ensure that there is no excess or lack of produce.

Now, take a look at the following diagram for a graphical representation of the Intelligent Automation levers at play to automate the Produce to Consume process:

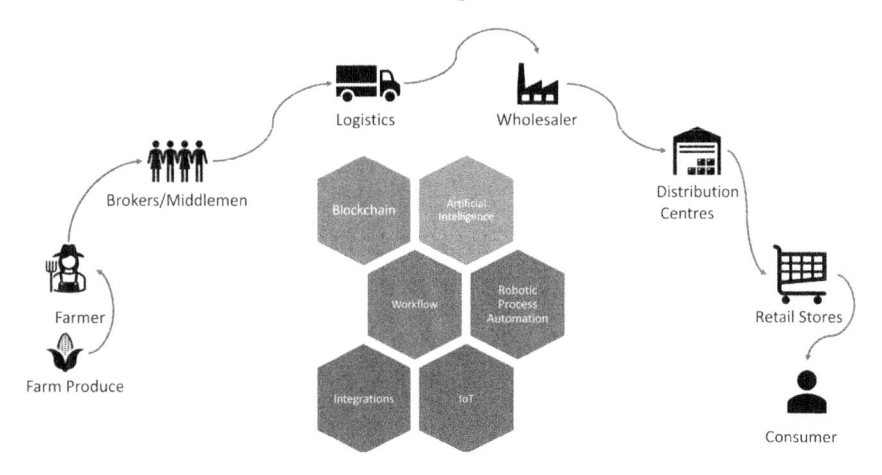

Figure 4.8: *Intelligent Automation Levers at Play to Automate the Produce to Consume process*

Though we have depicted this very simplistically, this, in fact, is an overly complex process. It is important to note how the individual technology pieces are tackling parts of the whole problem statement. Breaking down further, the retail and distribution processes will have workflows. The workflows will integrate with the other peripheral systems in the supply chain ecosystem to provide the right data needed to execute the workflow. There may be activities that will not be possible to implement through system integrations and might need an RPA bot to mimic the human actions. Thus you see the pieces of the puzzle, or the levers of Intelligent Automation fall into place and rightfully converge to drive the business benefits.

In reality, this process, which we described and solutioned very simplistically, is the crux of the supply chain. This whole process may not be automated in one single go – it would be too complex and impractical to do so. In a real-life scenario, such a process automation engagement would be broken down into smaller chunks and built iteratively. Just ponder over the process and the technology levers and try to align it with the concept of Intelligent Automation that we described in *Chapter 1, Introduction to Intelligent Automation*.

Before I summarize and conclude, I want to stress on the fact that such use cases are all around us, prevalent in all the industries and in our day-to-day lives. The need for process automation today is real and thriving. That's where the opportunity is. There is a strong push for operational efficiency in all the domains and spheres and that is driving the transformation to a hybrid workforce.

Conclusion

In this chapter, we discussed all the primary technology levers that constitute Intelligent Automation. We also discussed in detail all the technological components, starting from *Chapter 2, Robotic Process Automation, Chapter 3, Artificial Intelligence* and concluding them in *Chapter 4, Other technologies in Automation*. We understood the process characteristics that make a process fit for automation by each of these levers. We also discussed and appreciated the need to understand the business alignment with the non-technical criteria, and why it is important to build a business case to justify the RoI from automation. This completes the first section of this book.

With that said, now that we understand how to deliver Intelligent Automation, in the next chapter, we will focus on a few use cases from industries like Banking, and domains like IT Operations. We will define and elaborate the use cases and the high-level solutions, which you can take as an initial blueprint and use in your engagements.

References

1. Blockchain Overview: **https://www.ibm.com/in-en/blockchain/what-is-blockchain**

2. World Economic Forum Report: **https://reports.weforum.org/digital-transformation/the-internet-of-things-and-connected-devices-making-the-world-smarter/**.

3. Santander launches block chain : **https://www.globalbankingandfinance.com/santander-launches-the-first-blockchain-based-international-money-transfer-service-across-four-countries/**

4. Axa turns to smart contracts : **https://www.businessinsider.com/axa-turns-to-smart-contracts-for-flight-delay-insurance-2017-9?IR=T**

5. Enterprise Integration Patterns : **https://www.enterpriseintegrationpatterns.com/**.

CHAPTER 5

Intelligent Automation Use Cases

Introduction

In this chapter, we will discuss the Intelligent Automation use cases. We discussed a lot of theory around what is Intelligent Automation and how RPA and AI are key to implementing Intelligent Automation. Before we proceed to understand how to implement Intelligent Automation in an enterprise, let us discuss a few key use cases in detail and how the Intelligent Automation solution for them will appear. The previous chapters discussed a lot of theory and, by now, you are probably ready to jump into the field and get your hands dirty. So, in this chapter, we will take an industry like Banking and a domain like IT Operations. These are usually considered as the prime areas for automation. For these areas, we will discuss in detail a few large, grained processes, and the associated Intelligent Automation use cases in these areas.

We will discuss the typical pain points of the process and high-level process description, keeping it nonspecific to any enterprise context and analyze the use case to identify the areas of automation, as well as the potential levers of automation. Based on these requirements, we will define a high-level solution architecture to implement the use case. Since we will discuss the process at a generic level, we will make a few assumptions about the process, keeping the flavor of Intelligent Automation intact. The purpose is to provide you with a set of ideas and high-level solutions that you can take to the field and leverage in your day-to-day work.

Structure

In this chapter, we will cover the following topics:

- Introduction to the use cases
- Automation in the Banking and **Know Your Customer** (**KYC**) use case
- Automation in the IT Operations and Ticket Management use case

Objectives

After studying this chapter, you will be able to talk about some of the key Intelligent Automation use cases end to end. You will also be able to understand the high-level process for each use case, the automation potential and automation levers, and a high-level technical solution for each. You will be able to understand and implement the thinking process that goes in as you start creating the Intelligent Automation Solutions for real life use cases. You will also be able to follow and replicate the step-by-step activities starting from process identification, process detailing, identification of automation opportunities, and building the technical solution.

Introduction to the Use cases

As you have learnt by now, each automation lever is suited for automating a process based on certain criteria. **Robotic Process Automation** (**RPA**) can automate those processes that have a set of specific criteria as discussed in *Chapter 2, Robotic Process Automation*, and **Artificial Intelligence** (**AI**) can automate those processes that match a different set of criteria that we discussed in *Chapter 3, Artificial Intelligence in Automation*. In *Chapter 4, Other Exponential Technologies in Automation*, we discussed the criteria for applying the other exponential technologies. As we combine these different criteria, the possibility of automation really becomes large, and the identified levers can truly be diverse. So, as you can see, with the convergence of technologies that result in Intelligent Automation, the possibilities are enormous.

To substantiate all that we have learnt and discussed, in this chapter, we will discuss three processes – which can be considered as the three complex use cases. We will start with analyzing the process, identifying how the process can be automated, and discuss the technical solution to automate the same. We will also make a few assumptions while detailing out the process to avoid any specific enterprise scenarios, keeping the essence of the process intact that leads to the solution.

One use case is from banking – KYC management, and the other two are from the IT operations – Automated Ticket Creation and Automated Ticket Resolution.

We will discuss a few use cases from these key industries in the following format:

1. **Introduction to the use case**: A brief description of the scope of the use case and its associated pain points to the different stakeholders.

2. **High-level Process**: A high-level process flow identifying the broad activities.

3. **Detailed process view**: A textual description of the tasks and activities in the process with assumptions around specific IT systems, if any.

4. **Identification of the primary and secondary levers of automation**: Based on the detailed process description, the levers of automation will be marked.

5. **High-level solution diagram**: A high-level solution identifying the components of the solution.

6. **Detailed internal view of the selected automation components**: A detailed technical view of the selected automation components which are architecturally significant.

Use case in Banking

The Banking industry is one of the early adopters of automation. Banks have been facing challenges of high-operational cost, significant shift in customer expectations, and fintech disruptions, among others, which have led them to embrace automation earlier as compared to the other industries. Many large banks have already implemented the RPA based automation to automate the various back-office operations and are now into pilots and enterprise level implementations of Intelligent Automation initiatives across the globe.

While talking about Intelligent Automation, one of the common use cases that we have seen getting implemented is around Chatbots and Conversational AI for the various customer and business user facing interactions. However, there are multiple Intelligent Automation use cases in banking which are based on the complex processes and need multiple automation levers to be effectively automated.

In the following section, let us discuss one such use case which is part of one of the most essential and common processes in core banking, the KYC processing.

Use case 1: KYC Processing

Customer Onboarding is one of the essential processes in banking. It involves setting up new clients for the different banking services after successfully pursuing leads. One of the sub processes in Onboarding is KYC (Know Your Customer).

Introduction

KYC is an important process which assesses and evaluates the clients for setting up new accounts based on their identity verification, credit history, and risk profiles. This involves significant amount of data to be captured from the clients. There are various documents required as proofs of identity, profession, source of wealth, taxation, and so on, which need to be verified and validated through the various documents that are submitted. The associated data in the documents need to be checked against the authentic sources like the government data or financial agency data. The transaction history, political and economic profile of the customer, source of income and wealth and so on, are some of the checks that are essential to complete a KYC. The KYC is not only a regulatory compliance, but also an especially important process in risk assessment to ensure that the bank can identify the potentially risky customers and apply suitable control mechanisms to contain and mitigate that risk.

There are two aspects in the KYC process – customer identification and customer assessment. Customer identification is an important aspect of the KYC process where there is strict document verification to identify the customer. Once the identity is validated, the customer is assessed for his/her entire financial profile and beyond. The customer's financial history, professional and social profile, and any criminal activity is investigated and assessed. Is the customer a *"politically exposed person"*, does he/she have any economic or other sanctions at an individual or company level, are there any adverse reports in the press and media, and are there any evidence of a financial crime against the customer – all these are also assessed.

The process also includes a risk assessment based on the customer's profile, following which an overall risk profile is created. A higher risk profile of the customer exposes the bank to a higher risk of financial irregularities. Based on this, the customer is given the approval for onboarding and is set up for the different financial services offered by the bank.

High-level Process

The following diagram gives an overview of the KYC process as discussed:

KYC Request	Customer Identification	Customer Due Diligence	Enhanced Due Diligence	Customer Acceptance Decision
•Pull/Copy Customer Acquisition Data through various channels to create the KYC Request •Documents for Review	•Verify Name, Address, Unique Govt ID etc •Review and Validate Documentation	•Check is Politically Exposed •(PEP) •Check any Sanctions (individual, economic etc) •Risk Screening /Watchlists	•Special Checks and screenings if high risk individual	•Customer Risk Profile •Risk Category

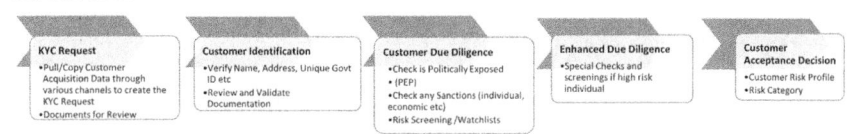

Figure 5.1: KYC Process Overview

In the preceding diagram, we have broken down the KYC process into several activities. The process starts when the KYC process is triggered after a successful lead is being converted to an account creation and set up. This typically involves the creation of a case or record in the KYC management process that will flow through the whole process and get enriched with the different verifications, assessments, and evaluations as per the KYC process. At the end, this case will have an approved, declined, or deferred decision, based on the overall risk assessed for the case.

As indicated earlier, customer identification is the first step in KYC. The customer identity is established based on the data and documents that the customer has submitted through the Account Opening process where the customer would be needed to fill in an Account

Opening Form and furnish the relevant data and proofs as required by the bank and regulatory policies. The data is usually captured in an enterprise CRM system as part of the process which is outside the scope of the KYC process. In our discussion, we will assume this data is already available for the KYC process.

In the next activity, which is generally known as **Customer Due Diligence**, the customer is assessed and investigated for the social, economic, and political exposures. The source of the customer's income and wealth is identified and assessed for any irregularities. The financial history of the customer is sought and assessed. There are checks to see if the customer has any economic sanctions and if he/she is on any economic, social, or security watchlist. Risk screening is done in which the external and internal data from the various internal and external sources like the government agencies or financial agencies is consolidated to create the risk profile. In case the result of Customer Due Diligence finds that the customer is potentially risky, then there are additional checks through Enhanced Due Diligence to further assess the customer and arrive at the risk profile. Finally, based on the assessment and evaluations, a risk category is predicted based on which the customer account is approved, deferred, or declined.

Detailed process view

Now that we have an overview of the process, let us understand the task level details of the process, so that we can identify what can be automated and how it can be automated. For the purpose of this book, we will do an assumption based deep dive into a use case, since the application system level details that will vary between each enterprise's implantation of the KYC process. Let us discuss each of the activities of *figure 5.1* in detail in the following section:

- **KYC Request**: Let us assume that there is a Lead Management system from where the request for KYC is pushed into the KYC Case Manager's mailbox or notified otherwise. The KYC Manager copies or pulls the data from the Lead Management System record and creates a new case for the KYC. This step, in many cases, could be a purely manual activity involving data copying between the systems.

- **Customer Identification**: Once the record is created in Case Manager, the KYC Manager starts the processing.

He/she validates the identity of the customer by verifying the documents submitted. He/she reads the data in the documents, extracts the data like the name, Government ID no., address etc., and verifies it against the internal and external sources through APIs, if available, or manually checking against the verified sources.

- **Customer Due Diligence and Enhanced Due Diligence**: Once the initial identity validation is done, the KYC Manager has to check against the internal and external resources to do the Customer Due Diligence, where the bank needs to identify and verify the source of the customer's money and wealth. So, the KYC Manager would need to conduct a screening by consolidating and evaluating the data collected from the various sources to build a risk profile for the customer. Typically, there could be specialized risk screening systems in the financial institutions to do this or there could be a mix of system-based assessment and human analysis to do the screening. Typically, the risk screening system will consolidate the data from the external and internal sources, structured and unstructured to create a single, consistent view of the customer profile data. If done manually, the KYC Manager will be doing a similar activity to consolidate data and build a single view of the customer. There are checks to see if a person is politically exposed and can have undue influence on the bank and financial transactions. There are also checks to see if there are any economic sanctions/financial litigations/adverse press against the customer. In case there is evidence for any of these, additional investigation and checks are done through Enhanced Due Diligence. To keep this use case simple, we will consider the basic Customer Due Diligence activity only.

- **Customer Acceptance**: Based on the risk profile, the KYC Manager will assess the risk potential of the customer as high, medium, low, and approve, defer, or decline the KYC request, and update the Case Manager with recommendations like Approve, Decline, or Request More Information.

Now that we have analyzed the process at the level of tasks, let us understand how to automate the process and what levers can be applied.

Identification of the primary and secondary levers of automation

Let us identify the different levers of automation and the automation opportunities. In *figure 5.2*, the callout briefly indicates the automation that is needed and the lever of the automation that could be applied. This is based on the nature of the process that we discussed earlier and the application of the criteria for automation fitment discussed in *Chapters 2: Robotic Process Automation,* Chapter 3: *Artificial Intelligence* and Chapter 4: *Other technologies for Automation.*

Now, take a look at the following diagram to identify the different levers of automation and the automation opportunities:

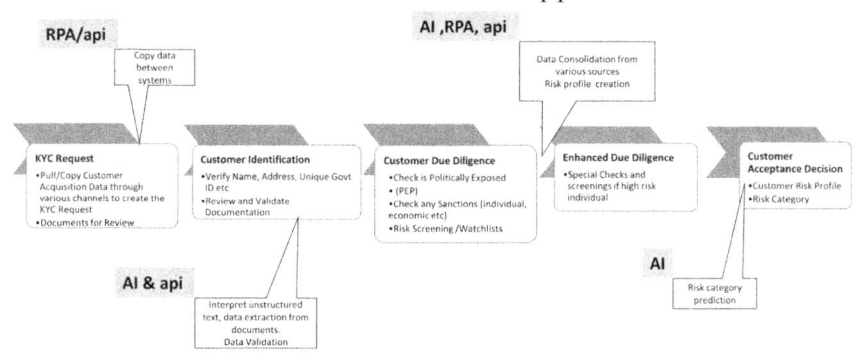

Figure 5.2: Automation Opportunities and levers of automation

Evidently, this use case has a mix of AI, RPA, and API based integration to build an Automated KYC Management system. Let us now list down the automation opportunities that have emerged from this, as follows:

1. **Creating the KYC Case with data from the Account Opening Form, Lead Management system**: This could be an API based integration to copy the data from the other systems to create the KYC Case. In the absence of APIs or a complex data copying requirement, this would be an RPA use case.

2. **Data Extraction from Documents**: The customer typically has to submit several documents, and specific entities from those documents usually need validations. An AI based document extraction to extract the relevant entities and an API invocation to the respective systems with the extracted data for validation would be able to automate a significant part of this activity.

3. **Data Consolidation from various systems and Building the Risk Profile**: For the first part, it could be a mix of RPA, AI, and API to consolidate the data from the various external and internal sources and create a single source of truth for the customer. For the second part, an AI based Risk prediction model would help in assessing the risk of the customer based on the customer profile created.

With these automation opportunities identified, let us now try to see the high-level solution that we can build on the basis of these requirements.

High-level solution diagram

Let us now look at a high-level Intelligent Automation Solution that we have created based on the preceding process, keeping in mind the identified requirements for automation and applying the suitable automation levers. The following diagram shows the components that will be used in implementing the Intelligent Automation Solution:

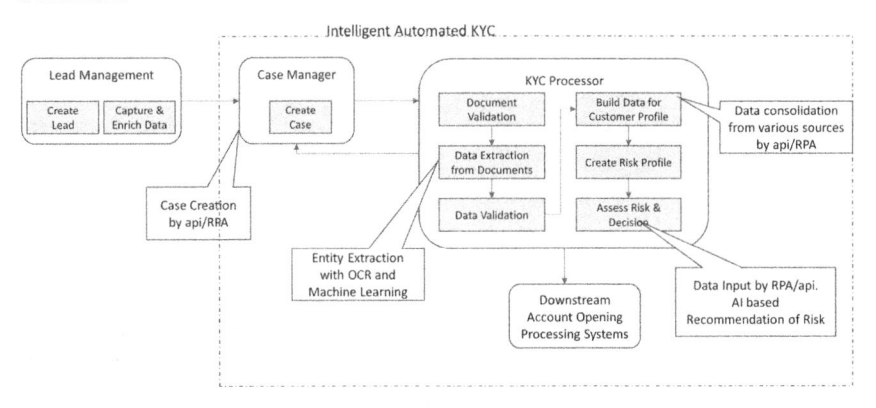

Figure 5.3: High-level Solution for Automated KYC Management

As you can see, in the preceding diagram (*figure 5.3*), the callouts against the components give you a brief idea about the function of the component. In a real engagement and implementation, this component model will be appended by the actual system names and with product/technology details. In the following section, we will dive deeper into these components to understand how their function and the technical sub-components are needed to implement them.

Detailed internal view of the selected automation components

Let us consider the components by their functionality groups as indicated in *figure 5.3*.

Automation 1: Case Creation Automation by RPA or API

The Lead Management System will send out a notification or trigger to initiate the KYC process. Typically, it is an email notification to the KYC Manager to start looking at a particular case. In the traditional process, the KYC Manager will look up the customer record in the Lead Management system and copy the relevant data into the Case Manager, ensure that the mandatory details are there, copy the relevant documents, and create the case. This is a manual activity, very repetitive, and could take somewhere between 5–20 minutes per case. This can be easily automated, either through the API based integration with the Case Management system or by RPA. In the automated scenario, there would be an RPA bot which will be triggered as a notification for the KYC generated. The bot or API integration would pull in the necessary data and documents from the Lead Management System or CRM systems and create a new KYC case for the customer. Take a look at the following diagram to understand the creation of KYC Case using API or RPA bot:

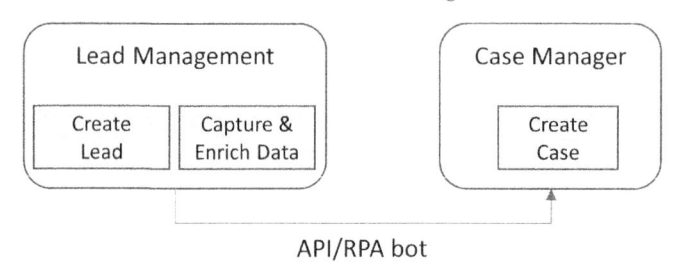

Figure 5.4: Create KYC Case

Automation 2: Data Extraction from PDF/image documents

After the Case is created, the KYC Manager needs to validate the identity of the customer. This will include integration with the external and internal systems like verification of Government ID, address, and so on. These are usually already automated with APIs. The part which is mostly manual in the process are reading and extracting the data from the submitted documents and then validating that data against the verified external or internal sources. The documents are usually submitted as PDF or image files or converted to PDF or images by scanning physical hard copy documents.

The document extraction from the PDF/images is our second automation and is not a very uncommon one. We are discussing this in context to KYC, but a similar solution can be used in automating similar use cases where you need to extract the data from the documents – native documents or PDF and images.

This use case will involve two things. One is to extract the data entities based on OCR plus entity recognition and natural language understanding (either as key value pairs or annotations) during the KYC processing. The second is to create a machine learning model that will do the entity recognition and natural language understanding, trained with the correct ontology. The second part is typically a one-time activity for a use case for a specific type of data, and might need periodic refinements if there are minor changes in the data. The first part is more on the operational data in hand and will be a runtime capability of the use case, where it will leverage the model that has already been built.

As you can see in *figure 5.5*, there is a file crawler that can pick the documents, for example, the PDF/image files stored in a predefined location, do any cleansing and noise reduction that may be needed, and then proceed with the entity recognition and related text extraction with the help of the machine learning model. For those entities that cannot be strictly classified and extracted as key value pairs, we could use the annotators to annotate the relevant sections that would provide guidance to the KYC Manager. The extracted entities and annotations would be stored in a data store from where it can be picked up for validations. The API based data validation is not shown separately here since it is pretty simple and straightforward. Take a look at the following diagram to understand the data extraction architecture:

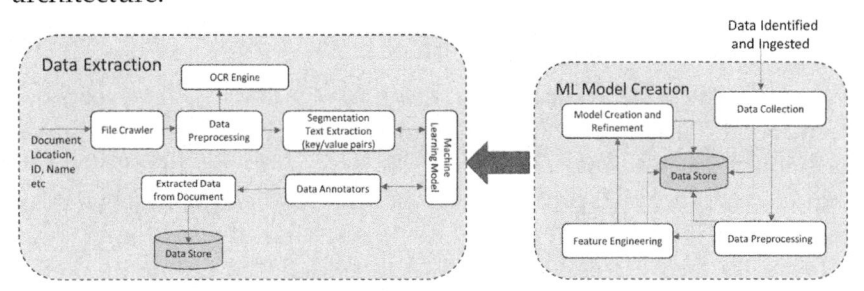

Figure 5.5: Data Extraction architecture

The other part of this use case is building the machine learning model that will do the entity recognition and annotations. This would need a typical machine learning pipeline where the related and relevant data, based on which the model will be defined and trained, is ingested, processed, any enhancements in terms of features to qualify and label the data is done, and a suitable algorithm is applied to build a model. There are different AI frameworks and products in the market which can recommend the top algorithms that will fit the data, or you could (based on your understanding of the data and the associated label) choose the best algorithm to build the model. It is recommended that, initially, you could go with the recommended algorithm that your product is suggesting and then refine it from there, if needed, until you have substantial experience.

Post the data extraction from the documents, this data is verified through the core systems existing in the enterprise.

Automation 3: Consolidate data from various internal and external sources and build the single customer view

The next activity would be to create a single view of the customer to enable a risk assessment. This could be done through a system or semi manually. If the risk screening is done through a system, this would mean entering a lot of data into the screening system from the Case Manager and the other systems if needed, which can be automated through RPA. If the data aggregation and screening is done manually, there would be a need to consolidate the data from the external and internal sources to build the profile. There can be diverse sources like Moodys, Factiva, Sources for Adverse Press, Sanctions, etc., in addition to the internal sources to get the transaction history, sources of income, etc. This can be done by an RPA bot plus a web crawler depending upon the various sources of data, in addition to any APIs that might help consolidate any data.

Automation 4: Risk Assessment

Based on the data aggregation from the various diverse sources mentioned earlier, an ML algorithm can apply various techniques like entity recognition, key value pair extraction, or annotations to build a customer risk profile. Based on this profile, the ML algorithm can predict the Risk category or Risk potential of a customer. This is basically the outcome of the KYC process. Based on the predicted risk, the downstream process to approve or reject the application for a new service can be invoked accordingly.

The following diagram provides a high-level overview for the Risk Assessment solution:

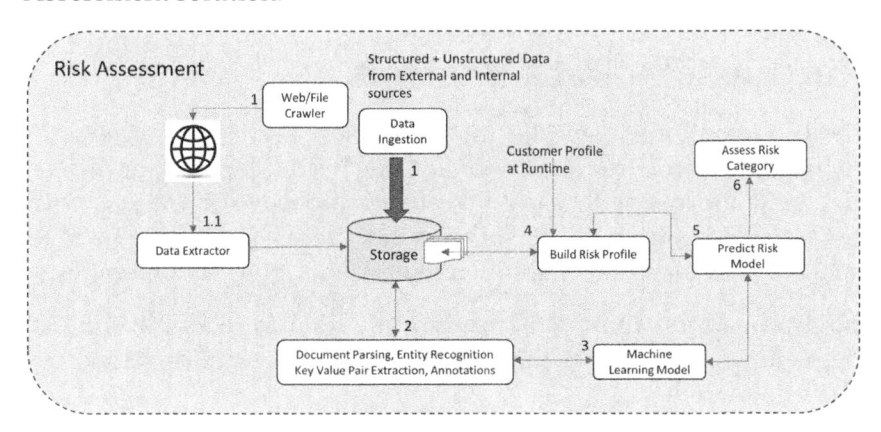

Figure 5.6: Risk Assessment solution

In the preceding sections, we have created an automation solution of a key process in Banking. We have, of course, simplified the process and made it generic for the purpose of this book. However, this will provide you with a general idea on how to go about creating the solution and a broad idea on how the solutions look like. We have not considered any tools, products, and frameworks for this solution yet.

Now that you have a conceptual solution created for the Intelligent Automation of a KYC system, you could take each component and identify the products/tools/frameworks that could be used to implement the solution. You could use any appropriate tool like UiPath, Blue Prism, Automation Anywhere, Microsoft Power Automate, etc., for the RPA. For AI, you could use the AI platforms and services offered by Google, Microsoft Azure, IBM Watson, AWS AI services, and others. You could also use the open-source frameworks and Python libraries that are available depending on your requirements – both technical and price wise.

Another important consideration, which is applicable for building all types of technical architecture is of the non-functional requirements. Here, we shall not consider any NFR specifically since they are very contextual, but that should be taken into account while you are designing the solution in real engagements, and NFRs would definitely impact the hosting of the automation solution.

A short section on hosting has been added at the end of the three use cases, later in this chapter, to provide you with some guidelines and direction of thought.

Use case 2: Automated Service Request/Ticket Creation

The IT Operations is getting more complex day by day. There are applications, infrastructures, and data that need to be managed across diverse platforms, with a need to ensure proactive operations with minimum downtime. On the other hand, there is a pressing need to save cost and increase reliability and efficiency of the IT Operations.

Intelligent Automation is the need of the hour to modernize the IT Operations and improve the efficiency, reliability, and productivity of the operations.

Introduction

Let us now consider a quite common use case for ticket or incident creation.

The business users send emails to helpdesks or customers send emails to Customer Service complaining about any dissatisfaction in the service. It could be the unavailability of a service, slow performance, wrong transaction, request, address change, and so on. This can be part of the business operations and the IT operations. The channel can be emails, chats, social media interactions, or phone calls. Such processes in the enterprise have issues around cycle time, dependency on agents and SMEs, and in some cases, significant customer dissatisfaction.

If you see, there are primarily three parts in this process which are typically manual and laborious. In the first part, the agent reads the email chat or listens to the voice message to understand what made the business user write such an email, chat, message and what their intent was. Once that interpretation is done, the agent must identify what additional data is present in the request like the customer number, account number, transaction ID, address etc. So, in the second part, he/she enriches the intent with additional data. For example, if the intent is identified as *"wrong transaction posted"*, the enriched intent would be supplemented by the transaction ID, transaction date, customer ID, account ID etc. Based on this, in the third part, he/she identifies the SOPs to take this forward. This would include creating a Service Request or Ticket, assigning it to the correct resolver group, and notifying the complainant.

Now, based on this high-level process, in the following few sections, we will take you step by step, explaining the rationale on how to go about automating this use case.

High-level Process

The following diagram represents a high-level process of what we discussed as the Service Request/Ticket Creation from the front end channels:

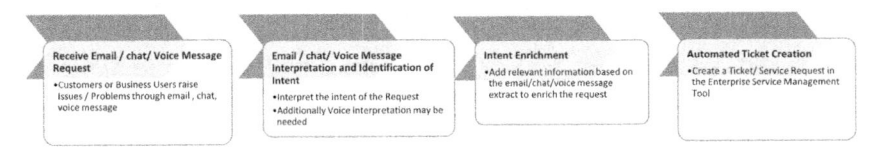

Figure 5.7: Ticket Creation from Email/chat and other communication

As you can see, we have broken down the process into four activities through which the complaint/issue/query is received and analyzed, and the relevant action to log it as a service request is done.

In the first activity, the actor is the business user or end user who is sending the email, chat, or voice message. The primary expectation for the actor in this process is that the email/chat should reach the right person and the action is immediately triggered towards resolution. The other expectation is that the user is notified of the status of his/her complaint.

In the following three activities, the primary actors are the agents at different levels who have the task of reading the email/chat and understanding the problem, and based on that, creating the relevant ticket. The additional value that the agent can offer to the process is to capture as much information from the email/chat and update the request for faster processing. We have all faced such situations where despite sending information through emails to the service providers or while talking to an operator, we need to repeat the information. This results in a lot of frustration at the customer's end, and needless to say, increases the cycle time of the complaint/issue handling. The activities start when the agent receives the note from the end user in a mailbox, does the requisite processing and analysis, and ends when he/she creates a ticket in the ticketing system. The next part of the process, which is the resolution of the ticket, will be handled in the following use case.

Detailed Process

Let us now understand each of the activities in detail, as follows:

1. **Activity 1**: The Email/Chat/Voice request from the end user (business or consumer) is sent to a common mailbox which is managed by the service agents. Typically, such emails/chats have a lot of emotions embedded along with the actual problem description, associated data related to the customer ID, transactions, plans, and other details.

2. **Activity 2**: The agent managing and monitoring the mailbox or the Email/Chat/Voice requests reads the email and understands the main complaint that the note or chat is conveying. Based on this, he/she may categorize the ticket and assign to a specific resolver group.

3. **Activity 3**: Based on the cause of the complaint that he/she has identified, the agent then tries to extract the other important details like Customer ID etc., if available in the note based on the SOPs. If the agent can identify the customer as a high net worth or a privileged customer, the appropriate identification is marked. Also, what could be of value is, if the agent can identify the tone or mood of the customer (say a very angry customer), he or she can mark it to be assigned to a priority queue.

4. **Activity 4**: The agent then logs into the Service Management System and logs a relevant ticket in the system with all the data that he/she has analyzed and identified, based on the email/chat, and assigns to the relevant resolver group.

Like the previous use case, the deep dive is generic since the process will be specific to an enterprise and will include many additional steps. We have tried to generalize and make it meaningful as far as possible while conveying the key ideas in the context of Intelligent Automation.

Identification of the primary and secondary levers of automation

The following diagram highlights the criteria based on which the automation levers are identified in this process:

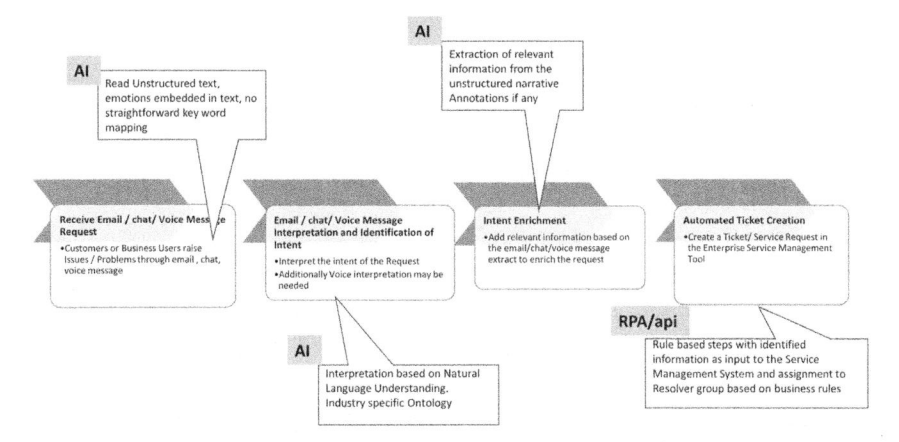

Figure 5.8: Identification of Automation Levers for Automated Ticket Creation

As you can see, for the first three activities, there is a significant amount of unstructured text interpretation, intent identification based on natural language understanding, data extraction from unstructured text, and tone identification which can be implemented by the different AI components. In the previous activity, it was a rule-based and well-defined one, where you knew which application you had to use to create the ticket, what data you had to input, and what buttons or controls you would have to click to create a ticket. This is an RPA use case, or depending on the Service Management tool that is being used, it could also be an API based integration to create the ticket.

High-level Solution

Now that we have understood the process at an activity and task level and identified the automation levers, we have sufficient information as requirements to create the high-level solution.

130 ■ *Intelligent Automation Simplified*

In the following diagram, you can see the main components that will be needed to implement this Intelligent Automation Solution:

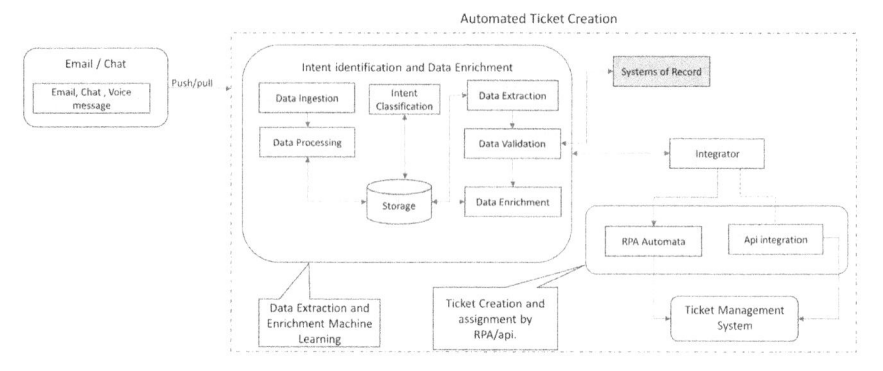

Figure 5.9: Component Diagram of Automated Ticket Creation

Let us now understand the functionalities of each of these components, as follows:

1. **Data Ingestion Component**: This will get the email/chat/voice messages by push or pull mechanism as per the requirements of the process. It will do pre-processing on the data which will include noise reduction and normalization (but not limited to these only) before it can be processed for Intent classification.

2. **Intent Classification**: The intent classification component will classify the emails/chats etc. and predict the customer's intention or purpose. For example, the intents could be update customer information, cancel transaction, change plan etc. The classification model will depend on the data that we have in hand and the categories that we must group the data into, based on the business requirements. Additionally, we could also enhance the classification model with the ontology-based intent detection. This means that the AI model will be trained with specific industry and business terms that might have special connotations and classify accordingly to predict more accurate and relevant results.

3. **Data Extraction**: Post classification, once the emails/chats are grouped into their respective categories, the AI system will extract the relevant data from the text narrative that could be used to enrich the intent. This component will leverage the machine learning models to extract specific data, irrespective

of where it appears in the text. In case of data that may not have a direct key value pair mapping, portions of the data can be annotated to assist the agent. In such a case, there may be a need for human interventions to validate and finalize the extracted data.

4. **Data Validation**: Once the data is extracted, it needs to be validated. For example, a customer might send an email requesting a service for which he or she may not be eligible. Or consider a case where the customer is complaining of an erroneous transaction with an invalid transaction ID. So, there is a need to validate a part or whole of the extracted data against the enterprise systems before passing it for the downstream processing.

5. **Data Enrichment**: Data validation and data enrichment will both leverage the data from the systems of record in the enterprise. The data enrichment component will pull out the additional data that may be needed to complete the customer's request as indicated in the email and aggregate for the ticket creation.

6. **Integrator**: Once the data is extracted, validated, and enriched, it is ready to be added as a Ticket/Service request. The Integrator component will identify the service endpoint that needs to be invoked for the same. The integrator component provides a lot of flexibility to configure what services need to be called to execute the next transaction. It provides a great mechanism to orchestrate the execution by decoupling the service provider and consumer end points. This component thus confers a lot of flexibility and configurability to the whole architecture.

7. **RPA Automation**: This component is basically the RPA bot, exposing a service endpoint. The most leading RPA tools have the capability of exposing automata as REST APIs. The RPA bot will get the enriched data in a desired format and execute the steps of creating the ticket or service request in the Service Management tool of the enterprise.

8. **API Integration**: This component and the RPA component may or may not be used together. Either the RPA bot will create the ticket or if the API based integration is available for ticket creation, it may be an API call to create the ticket. It

could also be a combination of the API and RPA automation, if required, to create the ticket, but the integration needs to be built in.

Detailed internal view of selected automation components

Now that we have discussed the components and their functions, let us take a closer look into the AI components for Intent Classification and Data Extraction. This will involve the machine learning models.

The first model will classify the requests based on the desired categories. The second model will aid in the relevant data extraction based on the ontology and natural language processing. There is another component, which is the speed to text component. This will take the voice messages as input and convert it into unstructured text that can be taken for classification. There will be pre-processing in terms of noise reduction needed for this type of data. In another variation of this solution, you can include a Tone Analysis AI component – a component to analyze the tone and mood of the end user. This component can provide insights on the mood of the user. Why this is important is because, in case a customer is terribly angry or frustrated, it may result in the customer cancelling the service and resulting in customer churn. So, if we can detect such extreme tones in the customer communication and take proactive actions by offering him priority services or special offers, it might result in better customer service.

The following diagram explains a few of the subcomponents that we have discussed; the Tone Analyzer is not shown here, as we considered it as optional:

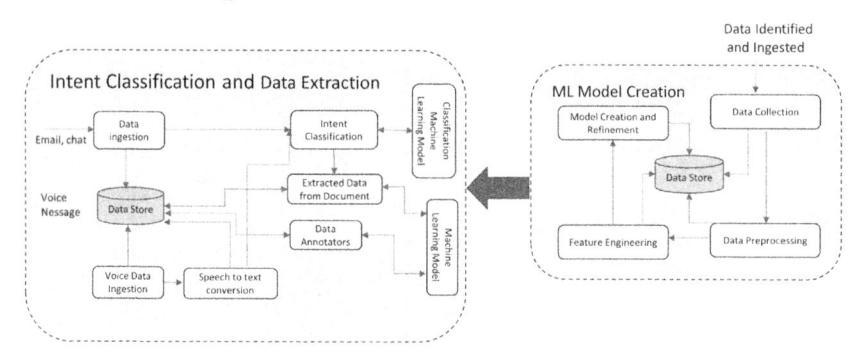

Figure 5.10: Classification and Data Extraction Detail diagram

This use case will end with a successful ticket creation in the enterprise ticket management system. Now that we have discussed the automated ticket creation, let us go to the next use case – a logical process, which is Automated Ticket Resolution.

Use case 3: Automated Ticket Resolution

This use case is again a quite common one in the context of IT Operations, and can be considered to be a continuation of the previous use case. Hence, this use case will start where the previous one ended.

Introduction

In use case 2, we discussed the situation about creating a ticket automatically, based on the different inputs through email, chat, voice message. In this use case, we will discuss how we can automate the ticket resolution.

Let us consider a typical process of ticket resolution. Once a ticket is raised in the Ticket Management system, it is classified based on the nature of the ticket, applications/processes impacted, and the other criteria. This classification may be done manually or could be automatic, based on the rules depending on the maturity of the operations. Based on the classification of the ticket, it is assigned to a Level 1 agent, who interprets the ticket and resolves the same. If he/she is unable to resolve it, it will be assigned to a Level 2 agent. The Level 2 agent is equipped with more detailed knowledge to fix an issue and can apply the configurations/scripts etc. to fix the ticket. Once fixed, the agent updates the ticket and notifies the end user.

The typical pain points in this process are related to high cycle time, high volume of ticket per agent, tickets not being resolved at Level 1, and so on. The motivation for automation for this use case is primarily to induce a Shift Left movement, i.e., closure of tickets/incidents as close to their generation. This implies two things. First is to have the ability to auto resolve the tickets without agent intervention. Secondly, in case the ticket cannot be auto resolved, it should be able to be resolved at Level 1 that would have chatbots to help in the resolution. The final resort, in case the ticket is not resolved at Level 1, is to assign it to a Level 2 agent, who not only has another chatbot help but also, based on the actions suggested by the chatbot, automates or semi-automates the resolution action. Let us look at the typical process flow of the Ticket resolution.

High-level Process

The following diagram represents a high-level process Ticket Resolution, which is quite standard across the enterprises and mostly covered in the preceding section:

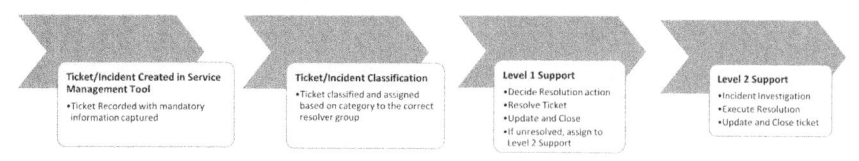

```
┌─────────────────────────┐  ┌─────────────────────────┐  ┌─────────────────────────┐  ┌─────────────────────────┐
│ Ticket/Incident Created │  │ Ticket/Incident         │  │ Level 1 Support         │  │ Level 2 Support         │
│ in Service Management   │  │ Classification          │  │ •Decide Resolution      │  │ •Incident Investigation │
│ Tool                    │  │ •Ticket classified and  │  │  action                 │  │ •Execute Resolution     │
│ •Ticket Recorded with   │  │  assigned based on      │  │ •Resolve Ticket         │  │ •Update and Close ticket│
│  mandatory information  │  │  category to the correct│  │ •Update and Close       │  │                         │
│  captured               │  │  resolver group         │  │ •If unresolved, assign  │  │                         │
│                         │  │                         │  │  to Level 2 Support     │  │                         │
└─────────────────────────┘  └─────────────────────────┘  └─────────────────────────┘  └─────────────────────────┘
```

Figure 5.11: High-level Ticket Resolution Process

As discussed, in the automated process, the goal is to have a significant Shift Left movement and get the ticket closed as close to the ticket creation. The ideal process should have the ticket auto classified, root cause predicted, resolution automatically recommended, and auto resolved based on the confidence score of the prediction.

Detailed Process

Let us now analyze the process in detail, taking each activity block one by one, as follows:

1. **Activity 1**: The Ticket/Incident request from the end user (business or consumer) is created through various channels. To create the ticket, there is a minimum amount of information that has be put into the ticket as mandatory information, like title, description of the issue, applications/processes impacted and others.

2. **Activity 2**: On the basis of the information available in the ticket, the classification is done according to the suitable categories prevalent in the enterprise. In the automated process, this would be the starting point for automation, with automated classification preferably not just based on the business rules, but with the AI based interpretation of the title and description of the ticket. After the ticket is classified, in the traditional process, it is assigned to the right resolver group and the right agent depending on the specific application/

process mapping with the resolver groups which is primarily rule based. In the automated process, this could also be an AI based prediction, based on the best agent available, his/her customer satisfaction ratings, skill level, and so on.

3. **Activity 3**: In the third activity, based on the ticket description and other associated data, the agent identifies the root cause of the problem and proceeds to identify the resolution action for the same. If the resolution action is in his/her scope of work, the ticket is resolved, else it is assigned to a Level 2 agent. In the to-be scenario, an AI component could predict the root cause of the ticket and recommend remedial actions based on the standard operating procedures, FAQs, Runbooks etc., on which it has already been trained on. If such an automation already exists in the system, it can be auto triggered, thus resulting in auto resolution of the ticket. Once the resolution action is auto executed, the ticket is updated and closed, and the user is notified of the resolution. If auto resolution is not present due to any constraint – may be unavailability of relevant automation – the agent can be assisted with a chatbot guidance that can recommend a possible resolution action, and also provide insights on how similar incidents have been resolved.

4. **Activity 4**: This activity occurs when the ticket gets assigned to a Level 2 agent. In a traditional scenario, the Level 2 agent will understand and analyze the ticket, validate the root cause identified by the Level 1 agent, and identify and execute the resolution. In the automated process, the goal is to resolve as many tickets as possible, either automatically or at the Level 1 stage. In case it moves to Level 2, there are two types of assisted automation that can happen. One is a chatbot assistance that will guide the agent on how to resolve the ticket and display similar occurrence and their resolutions. The second is, once the resolution is identified by the chatbot or by the agent manually, a bot can be triggered in an assisted or attended mode to perform the resolution.

Identification of the primary and secondary levers of automation

Like the previous use case, the deep dive is generic and based on assumptions, but this process is fairly standard and we have followed the traditional ITIL process to make it as close as possible to the real process. But, the interfacing systems like the Service Management system, mechanism and criteria, or threshold for the tickets to be pushed or pulled may be different and will be specific for a specific enterprise scenario.

The following diagram highlights the criteria of the activities in the process that has been a key in identifying the automation levers:

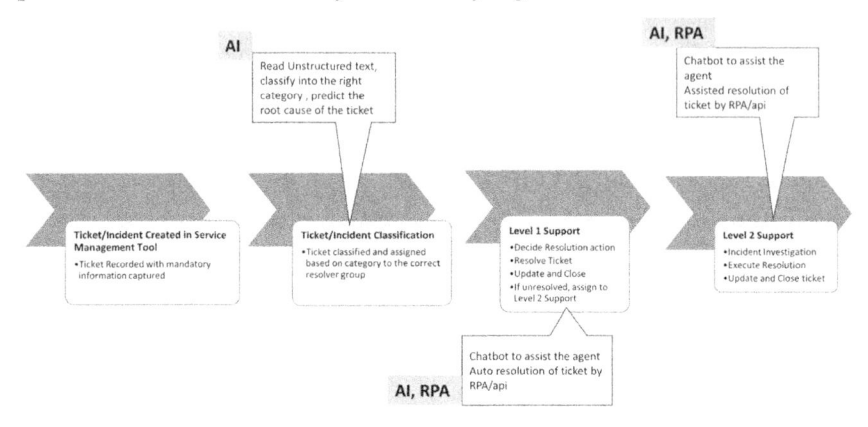

Figure 5.12: Automation Levers identified for Automated Ticket Resolution use case

As you can see, for each of these activities, there is a significant amount of unstructured text interpretation, intent identification based on natural language understanding, and data extraction from unstructured text which are different AI components. RPA or APIs will feature here for the execution of the resolution action only.

High-level Solution

Now that we have understood the process, activity, and tasks involved, and identified the automation levers, we have sufficient information as requirements to create the high-level solution.

In the following diagram, you can see the main components that will be needed to implement this Intelligent Automation Solution:

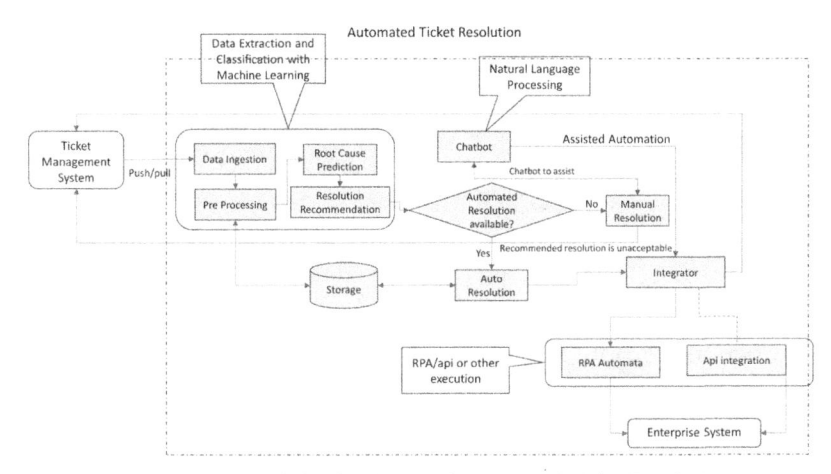

Figure 5.13: High-level solution of Automated Ticket Resolution

Data Ingestion Component: This is similar in nature to the component we discussed in the previous use case. This component will get the ticket data by push or pull mechanism as per the requirements of the process. It will conduct pre-processing on the data which will include noise reduction and normalization (but not limited to these) before it can be classified to identify the ticket categories in the classification component.

Root Cause Prediction: This component is a large-grained component. It will do two things – categorize the ticket and predict the root cause. In your solution, you can have them as separate components. For the sake of simplicity, it has been combined into one in this solution.

This component will classify the tickets based on the nature of the ticket. In the same component, the root cause prediction can also be done with the classification based on the different labels than the previous one. For example, a ticket can be categorized into a bucket called Supply Chain Tickets based on the application or processes impacted. The root cause could be predicted as unavailability of the correct item codes based on the machine learning model for the root cause prediction.

Additionally, we could also enhance the classification of the AI model with the ontology-based intent detection. This means that the AI model will be trained with specific industry and business terms that might have special connotations and classify accordingly to predict more accurate and relevant results.

Resolution Recommendation: This component will leverage an AI model trained on the different root causes and solutions that were applied to fix the root cause. Hence, this component will recommend the resolution actions with a confidence score. If the confidence score is beyond a certain threshold – say 85% or 90% , depending on the criticality of the issue, it can invoke the integrator for the auto resolution action. Typically, this threshold should be configurable since it might change for the different applications and business portfolios.

Now, once the resolution is recommended, there can be two options. One is auto resolution, where an automation already exists for the resolution recommended which can be automatically triggered. The other option would be that the resolution action needs to be executed manually because there is no automation available, or the resolution recommended by the AI component was below the acceptance threshold. In both cases, the ticket will be handed off to a human agent who can take the assistance of a chatbot to resolve the ticket with assisted automation. In case the chatbot is also not able to resolve, then the agent needs to ask for an SME help and manually resolve the ticket, as the last resort.

Integrator: This is the similar integrator component discussed in the previous use case. The Integrator component will identify the service endpoint that needs to be invoked for the ticket resolution. As discussed, this component confers a lot of flexibility and configurability to the whole architecture.

RPA Automation: This component is basically the RPA bot, exposing a service endpoint of the resolution action that needs to be executed. Most RPA tools have the capability of exposing the automata as REST APIs.

API Integration: This component and the RPA component may or may not be used together. The API integration is also another endpoint for the resolution action execution.

Detailed internal view of the selected automation components

Most of the components discussed in this solution have some commonalities with the previous use case and have already been discussed, except for the chatbot component. Let us now understand the high-level architecture of the chatbot component. The following diagram details out the high-level solution of a chatbot:

Chatbot Architecture

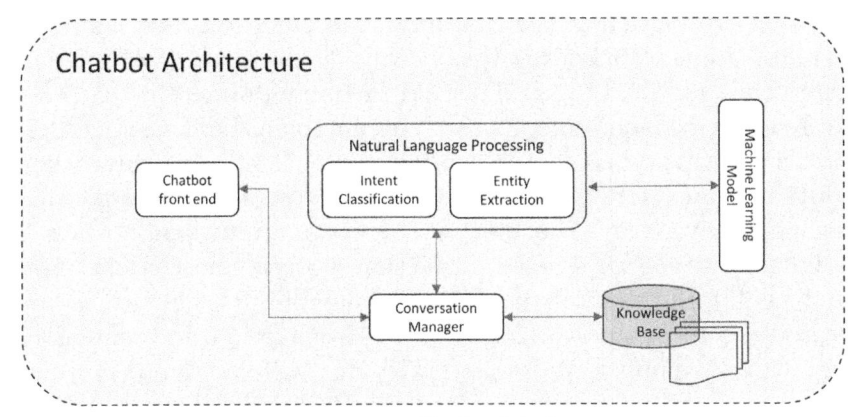

Figure 5.14: Chatbot Solution

This is not overly complicated and is mostly generic. You need to have a chat front end which could be a portal or an existing chat front end prevalent in the enterprise. The primary components are Natural Language Processing with Intent classification and entity extraction. There needs to be a conversation or dialog manager to conduct the dialog between the user and the system and direct the conversation such that, in case of ambiguities, more questions can be asked to the user to understand the correct intent.

In the back end, there is a knowledge base with curated corpus specific to the domain and intents that the chatbot will be handling in its scope. In this use case, the corpus will be curated based on FAQs, Runbook, past tickets and other sources of information that may be existing.

This use case, thus ends here, and before we end this chapter, there are a few more points to touch upon to add a closure to this topic.

Solution Realization of Use cases

By now, you have got a fair understanding of the different types of solutions that are commonly used, integration between AI and RPA/API and how the overall solution flows. There are two more things that we will discuss in this chapter before we end.

So far, in the solutions, there is no mention of any specific product, tool, or framework. However, we have touched upon the RPA and AI tools and services options in the preceding sections while discussing the use cases in detail. Apart from the ones mentioned here, there are a multitude of other options available for each component implementation. We have not selected any particular product of the tool in these solutions, because tool selection is often beyond the scope of any particular use case and is an enterprise decision. It is an automation platform discussion with technical, commercial, and compliance aspects to it, and should be rarely done at the use case level, unless the requirement is very specific and niche. The other topic to briefly touch upon is about the hosting of the Intelligent Automation solution. There can be many options. It can be a completely on-premise hosting, a private cloud hosting, or a hybrid or multi cloud hosting. It is difficult to generalize this topic because it is very much dependent on the enterprise's requirements, availability of infrastructure, nature of products and frameworks used in implementation, and regulatory compliance, amongst other criteria. So, this will vary from use case to use case, and enterprise to enterprise, and will be a very specific discussion that you need to conduct. The guideline for this is to capture your non-functional requirements as you are capturing the process automation requirements, assess the impact of the non-functional requirements on the automation components, and accordingly, decide on a suitable deployment model.

Conclusion

In this chapter, we discussed three incredibly significant use cases and their automation solutions. However, this is like a drop in the ocean. There is an abundance of use cases in all the industries and domains that can be automated with varying degrees of complexity. The idea of discussing these use cases in particular was to give you an end-to-end view and demonstrate the thinking process, while identifying the right use case and taking it step by step through the solution design. The other aspect that we wanted to bring out is the fact that Intelligent Automation is very real. In these common use cases, you saw a significant convergence of different technological components that were necessary to automate the processes and bring on Intelligent Automation.

In the next chapter, we will discuss, from a practical perspective, how typical Automation journeys look like, how do enterprises embark on such journeys, what the different starting points are, and what the key enablers are for such transformation. We will discuss the importance and need for a CoE, and what the scope of a CoE is in a typical Automation journey. The idea is that, in the first few chapters, you got a primer of the technology behind Intelligent Automation; in the later half, you will get the real life tips and examples on how to execute such a project with a client.

CHAPTER 6
Enterprise Automation Journey

Introduction

In *Chapter 1, Intelligent Automation*, we discussed how several technologies come together to enable end-to-end automation of a process in Intelligent Automation. In the chapters on the different technologies – RPA, AI, blockchain – we saw how Intelligent Automation is actually a convergence of technologies with the aim to automate a process end to end, and in the previous chapter you saw how we design an Intelligent Automation solution for a use case and detail out the various components.

In this chapter, we will discuss the enterprise automation journey for Intelligent Automation. We will discuss the aspects around how to start the journey, and then take it forward as an enterprise transformation. Most enterprises today have already started or have a plan to start their automation journey in the near quarters. However, though many of them have experimented with automation and have reaped some benefits, the large-scale automation adoption across enterprises is still elusive. We will discuss about the challenges for enterprise automation and talk about how they can be managed and resolved. We will discuss in detail, the scaling of automation by the adoption of a Centre of Excellence approach. With that in context, let us get started with the Enterprise Automation Journey.

Structure

In this chapter, we will cover the following topics:

- Challenges in Implementing Enterprise Automation
- Enterprise Automation Journey
- What is an Automation Center of Excellence?
- Why do we need an Automation Center of Excellence?
- Functions of a CoE
- Different Models of CoE
- How to set up a CoE?

Objective

After reading this chapter, you will be able to understand the journey that an enterprise needs to traverse for automation. You will get a glimpse of the real-life challenges in enterprise automation and what approaches can be adopted to mitigate and resolve those challenges. You will be able to understand the enterprise automation journey around how to start, how to traverse the various stages of automation, and scale as you traverse. You will be able to appreciate the need for and importance of a Centre of Competence in scaling automation in the enterprise, as you understand the functions of a CoE, and how the CoE brings together the business and IT stakeholders of the enterprise to build and deliver successful automation. At the end of this chapter, you will be able to recommend to your clients an approach to scale automation and create a roadmap for the Enterprise Automation Journey, outlining how to achieve that with the help of a Center of Excellence.

Challenges in Enterprise Automation

In *Chapter 1, Introduction to Intelligent Automation*, we discussed the different stages of automation – Basic, Intermediate, and Advanced. Each stage leverages the previous stage and sets the foundation for the next.

The enterprise automation journey follows a similar path. Intelligent Automation is difficult to achieve as a big bang approach and that is why we call it a journey. Most enterprises today have automation in some form or the other. There are workflows, scripts, macros, and batch processes that take some amount of manual and tedious work away from the humans and are executed automatically. According to the analysts, roughly 30% of the enterprises are at this stage, and the automation at this stage is primarily centered around task automation.

Typically, we have seen enterprises start with small automation proof of concepts and production pilots with workflows and RPA. Once the benefit with this type of automation is perceived, a consensus is built in the enterprise to scale it to more critical use cases. Next comes the converging of technologies. For example, once RPA is established, it makes sense to add AI with RPA to automate a suitable process, or use other integration techniques to achieve complete process automation.

However, things changed across the globe in 2020. With the pandemic disrupting our lives and the way we work, automation and digital transformation are one of the top priorities of CIO and COOs across the world. Digital Transformation with Digital Ecosystems are becoming key imperatives for the C-Suite Executives across industries. Automation is a key enabler for such enterprise-wide digital transformation. The discussions have moved from task automation to process automation, from workflows to smart and intelligent workflows. Automation is now an enterprise priority, a prime enabler of digital transformation.

In various conversations with clients regarding automation over the past few years, we have see that there are a few common topics that emerge around starting and scaling automation. There are common concerns around where to start automation, how to define the ROI of automation, and once the definition of ROI is established, how to achieve it. We have seen clients enquire about how to create a continuous pipeline of valuable and validated automation use cases once the low hanging fruits are gone. In most cases, it is the back-office operations use cases which they had started their automation with and most of these are usually implemented with RPA. So, how an enterprise moves from RPA to Intelligent Automation in a structured way is one of the questions that we will discuss in this chapter.

According to analysts, today, less than 10% of the enterprises have really built automation at scale, though a much larger percentage are significantly invested in it already. The enterprises are aware of the benefits of automation, have insourced or outsourced resources to build the automation, but still, when it comes to scaling automation, they face challenges at multiple fronts. In this chapter, we will discuss this journey in detail – how to plan and execute an automation transformation journey in an enterprise, what the key aspects are that we need to be aware of, what the best practices are, and how to handle the common pitfalls.

Let us first try to understand what the challenges in Enterprise Automation are.

There are some common challenges that the enterprises usually face in their automation journey, which is depicted in *figure 6.1*. Let us now understand how these challenges impact the automation journey of an enterprise, as shown in the following diagram:

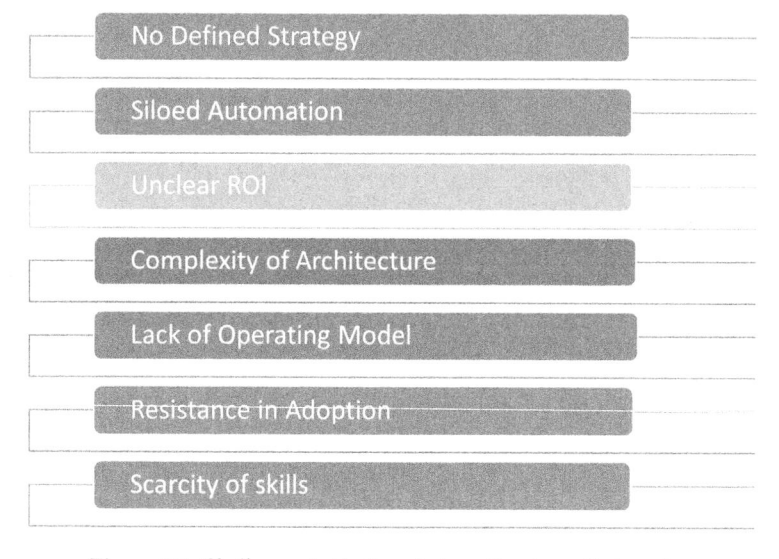

- No Defined Strategy
- Siloed Automation
- Unclear ROI
- Complexity of Architecture
- Lack of Operating Model
- Resistance in Adoption
- Scarcity of skills

Figure 6.1: *Challenges in Scaling Automation in an Enterprise*

Absence of a defined strategy

A well-defined automation strategy is especially important for a successful Enterprise Automation journey. Addressing questions like what the drivers of automation are and what benefits we want to achieve through automation is the key in designing the journey.

The strategy should provide the direction to what the enterprise wants to achieve by automation and a high-level blueprint of the journey to achieve it. It should provide guidance around the kind of opportunities that should be identified and prioritized, what the operating model should be to interact with business and IT, how benefits will be measured and fed back into the automation lifecycle, and who would be the key stakeholders for the automation journey. Clarity on these aspects pave the way for a clear and defined direction on how to create a continuous opportunity pipeline, how to go about building the automation for the identified opportunities, and eventually, how to build a self-sustaining automation organization within the enterprise. This needs to be a well thought-out exercise, bringing in all the key stake holders from the Business Units and the IT organization. A haphazard or half-baked strategy can seem to work when you start automating a few processes or the low hanging fruits, but as the enterprises scale automation, any delay in defining the strategy will only create more complexity and slow you down as the automation ecosystem moves forward.

Siloed Automation across enterprise

The large enterprises have various automation initiatives going on across the enterprise. Many a times, these may be isolated initiatives across the business units. Different business units have different priorities based on which, they might be at different stages of automation. These may be with diverse tools and technologies and may or may not be a part of a planned exercise. The probability of the latter is generally higher. This gives rise to the various isolated automation solutions with diverse tools and technologies, thus resulting in an enterprise architecture that becomes overly complex and inflexible as it progresses. The IT environments are inherently complex. On top of that, adding multiple tools for addressing similar type of work without a holistic enterprise view, raises the cost of ownership multiple times. This also results in siloed and fragmented automation, with maintenance nightmares, thus reducing the operational efficiency and defeating one of the main purposes of automation.

Unclear ROI

This is one of the key challenges when it comes to automation. In various discussions with the Automation Leaders across different industries, this is one of the most discussed topics. The ROI of automation becomes especially important since most automation initiatives need significant investment of time and money. As automation scales, there is a strong need to have a mechanism through which the ROI can be calculated, and a valid and justifiable business case can be created. We discussed this need to have a strong business case and predictable ROI while selecting the processes for automation in *Chapter 2: Robotic Process Automation, Chapter 3: Artificial Intelligence, and Chapter 4: Other Technologies in Automation*, and how the non-technical characteristics of the process become important in identifying the value that the process automation will bring in. The principle is to select the right processes for automation and prioritize them based on a combined weightage of technical criteria and the business value that the automation will bring in. Getting a view of the ROI during opportunity identification as well as monitoring whether the ROI is realized after deployment are the key aspects of a self-sustaining automation organization.

Resistance in Automation Adoption

One of the biggest challenges in scaling Intelligent Automation is the resistance from the employees and customers to the change. Intelligent Automation is bound to introduce some change in the way things work. We, as human beings, usually react to changes by either embracing them or resisting them. The most obvious unconscious reaction is the resistance before the slow acceptance. The resistance to automation comes from the fear of losing jobs for the employees, or the complexity of the change for the customers. The right amount of awareness about the change that automation will bring – both from the employee's and customer's perspective – can help embrace such significant shift in the organization. As a result, the right change management strategy to adopt automation is extremely important in making the Intelligent Automation journey successful in an enterprise. Having a readiness assessment, conducting awareness sessions, highlighting the benefits of automation, and how that will impact the employee and customer experience can go a long way in embracing automation.

Lack of an Operating Model

In an automation journey, it is especially important to define the right operating model. An Automation Operating model is the framework with people, process, and technology that determines how to deliver the right value to the enterprise through automation. Automation operates in a complex ecosystem of Business and IT – with the associated process, people, and technology. An operating model defines how the different stakeholders in the complex automation ecosystem will interact, participate, and collaborate, using the defined processes, methods, and tools. The lack of a defined operating model might result in uncoordinated or siloed automation across the enterprise, which might fail to generate the short and long-term benefits for which they were planned. Having an operating model will ensure that there is a defined framework through which the automation lifecycle is driven and generating the business value. The operating model defines how the automation opportunities are created, developed, and delivered, and are aligned to the overall automation strategy of the enterprise. An operating model helps the stakeholders to understand their roles and responsibilities, and how each of them contribute to the overall success of automation. Having a well-defined operating model streamlines and reduces the complexity of building the automation at scale in an enterprise.

Complex technology architecture

As we move through the different stages in Intelligent Automation, the automation capabilities are greatly enhanced, and the enterprise architecture becomes complex. The new tools, technologies, and products make their place in the ecosystem, and operating and managing them can become a challenge, if this is not planned properly. As technologists, we sometimes tend to over architect a problem. So, it is important to keep in mind that for any technical solution, there should always be a strong business driver. The technology that does not deliver the business benefit has little shelf life. An overly complex technological ecosystem can sometimes be a deterrent to scaling automation. This can however be managed with proper planning, flexible and scalable architecture, and skilled resources that can craft the solution landscape based on the business needs.

Scarcity of suitable resources

Intelligent Automation is made up of several technologies, and hence it requires a variety of skills, both from the technical and the business perspective. The typical roles would be the business analyst or process analyst, architect, developer, tester, data scientist, etc. Many of these, like the data scientists, are niche roles. While scaling automation, there can be times when you face a scarcity of these skilled resources. The architects, business analysts, process consultants, and developers are all in-demand skills, and there may be situations when the supply is less than the demand. To manage such situations, there needs to be a well-defined automation training and enablement plan. Proper planning, adopting a mix of insourced and outsourced skills and creating a capability and capacity roadmap to forecast and manage the demands ahead of time can help in addressing the problem of resource scarcity for automation.

These are some of the key challenges that the enterprises typically face while scaling automation. There can be others which may be very contextual to the enterprise based on their policies and strategies, which you may have to consider when you are working with a particular client scenario. Now that we have a fair understanding of some of the important challenges in enterprise automation, let us try to visualize what an automation journey could look like.

Journey Towards Intelligent Automation

Let us revisit the automation journey through the different stages that we discussed in *Chapter 1, Introduction to Intelligent Automation*. We have used the same visualization and tried to depict a typical journey of an enterprise. It starts with the basic automation primarily with scripts, macros, and some basic RPA for task automation, and slowly, as the technology proves itself, it moves on to activity and process automation with RPA. Then the journey continues to include the OCR, chatbots, ML, IoT, blockchain and others, as the enterprise matures and slowly moves towards Intelligent Automation at scale. Take a look at the following diagram for a better understanding of this journey:

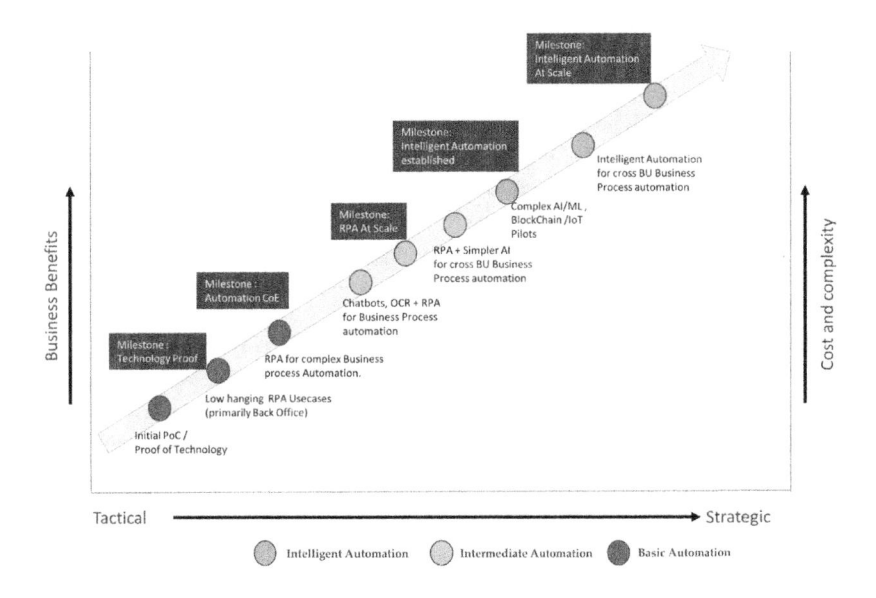

Figure 6.2: Enterprise Automation Journey

The journey depicted in the preceding diagram looks linear for the sake of simplicity. However, in a real enterprise, this will be a complex transformation which will involve massive shifts in people, process, and technology. As you can see in the preceding diagram, the whole journey has several significant milestones. Each milestone signifies the establishment of the automation goals as it scales. It starts from task automation to process automation, then moves from RPA to OCR, from chatbots to machine learning, and associated convergence. At each step, the technology needs to prove that it can deliver the promised business benefits and is reflected as the milestone, thus setting the foundation for the larger journey.

In the Intelligent Automation stage, there are two milestones depicted in *figure 6.2*. The first milestone is the establishment of Intelligent Automation, which means that there is a successful framework with underlying tools and technologies that enable the convergence of many technologies to automating a business process. The other milestone – Intelligent Automation at scale – indicates that the Intelligent Automation framework established is repeatable, optimized, and has successfully been applied to automate the enterprise wide processes making them smart, adaptable, self-serving, or self-healing.

Often in many discussions with the clients, we have come across this request to show what a typical automation journey looks like. This view described in *figure 6.2* is an overly simplistic view as mentioned already. However, it gives you the broad picture of how the journey will look like. The journey is driven by a strategic push to move from limited desktop automation to RPA to Intelligent Automation with the objective to deliver business value. The business value and outcome can be in terms of cost savings, improved efficiency, faster value realization, or improved employee or customer experience.

Once the technology is proven through the proof of concepts and pilots, it is important to define the automation strategy and the operating model. This is usually achieved by setting up a dedicated group to manage the overall automation strategy, lifecycle, and governance. This dedicated group may be referred to by various names like Automation CoE or Automation Factory. In this book, we will refer to it as Automation CoE. What is important to understand is the functions of this group and how that aids in scaling automation across the enterprise.

The underlying principles of the functioning of an Automation CoE, embody a well-defined collaboration between the business and IT to achieve a common goal as described in the automation vision of the enterprise. The Automation CoE enables a streamlined end-to-end automation governance lifecycle across the enterprise ecosystem. With that thought in mind, let us now dive deep into the Automation CoE and understand why it is important to set up such a dedicated group to drive the automation in an enterprise, and detail out what functions do they perform.

The Automation CoE thus, plays the role of the central driver for automation supported by the business and IT, as it transitions from RPA or other basic automation to Intelligent Automation, through convergence of chatbots, data extraction, image recognition, IoT, blockchain, and integration.

Automation Center of Excellence

Let us first understand what is a CoE or Center of Excellence?

Usually, a CoE refers to an entity within an organization that provides specialised services for a specific technology or domain. The services include thought-leadership, evangelisation, governance, best practices, delivery support, training, and so on, for the selected area. We need to build a CoE when there is a need to develop new expertise in a specific area and manage the growth organically. You have probably seen such CoEs in your own organization or client organizations that you are working with.

Need for Automation Center of Excellence

Now, the next question is why do we need a CoE? In short, in the context of automation, CoEs are needed to overcome many of the challenges of enterprise automation that the organizations face as they try to build and scale automation to deliver business benefits. We have discussed many of these challenges in the previous section. In the following few sections, we will understand how a CoE addresses those challenges and more.

As you have seen, an unclear strategy is one of the big roadblocks in the automation journey. The Automation CoE starts with the definitions of the vision, mission, and goals for the enterprise with respect to automation. The CoE defines and lays down the key drivers of automation and what the enterprise wants to achieve via automation. This is also aligned with the broader business goals of the enterprise, and CoE becomes an enabler in that space. The vision and objectives provide guidance to the CoE charter and influences the design of the CoE.

Siloed automation, a key challenge as discussed, results in fragmented systems and a tunneled automation approach. The ecosystem becomes difficult to maintain and manage and the cost of ownership subsequently increases. There is usually no common framework, platform, and governance for automation, and this usually proves detrimental to the overall benefit of automation in the long run. Automation CoE plays an important role in bridging the siloes and creating an overarching umbrella for providing guidance, leadership, and governance in the automation ecosystem. Depending on the type of operating model, the CoE is able to provision the right kind of ownership and control between the business and IT groups in the enterprise with respect to automation. We will discuss the CoE operating models in a later section of this chapter.

You may be able to appreciate that ROI and benefit tracking are especially important when it comes to automation, and one of the most common drivers of automation is cost savings. So, there needs to be a mechanism to select those processes for automation that will generate significant ROI, and once these processes are automated and deployed in production, the benefits need to be tracked and measured. An efficient mechanism for the preceding points is key to the success of automation in an enterprise. One of the key functions of CoE is to be able to define the mechanism and tools to capture, track, and monitor the automation benefit. This mechanism goes a long way in making automation a self-sustaining organization within the enterprise.

Depending on the enterprise structure, its automation vision, and the way the business and IT work together in the enterprise ecosystem, Automation Centre of Excellence can have different operating models. Depending on the enterprise construct, a CoE can be part of the IT organization, or part of the Business Organization, or a separately funded unit. Whatever the model is, it is important to have the CoE operating model laid out and agreed upon by the business and IT stakeholders for the automation to be successful. A view of this construct is usually defined in the operating model of the CoE.

Apart from providing guidance and thought leadership, CoEs are also key in spreading awareness in the enterprise about automation, demonstrating the power of automation, and how it will impact the employee and customer experience. These have significant impact on reducing the resistance to change and appreciating the benefits of automation in an enterprise. With the overarching governance, the CoE also helps in managing the technological complexity and bringing in uniformity in the automation ventures with the enterprise-wide principles and policies that need to be adhered by any automation initiative from the business or IT. People enablement is also one of the areas in the CoE charter, and there is always special focus on how to build the skill and knowledge on automation within the enterprise, thus mitigating the risk of the scarcity of resources. There are usually the CoE driven initiatives to build the specific role-based skills depending on the demand-supply outlook of the enterprise automation.

Thus, we see that the typical challenges that the enterprises face while scaling automation is mostly contained and reduced to a great extent with the setup of an Automation CoE. And that is why, it is key that as automation scales, a CoE is set up to drive it with strong leadership, focus, and governance.

By now, there may be a third question that might have arisen in your mind. Who or what kind of organizations need an Automation CoE? CoE might sound like a heavy or loaded term, it might sound like something that belongs to the large enterprises with a multimillion-dollar automation investment. However, regardless of the size or industry, all kinds of enterprises can benefit from an automation CoE. There is no one-size-fits-all. The CoE should be designed carefully, keeping in mind the enterprise's construct, automation vision, drivers, and the outcome it strives to achieve.

To summarize, the Automation CoE plays a key role, when it comes to scaling automation – be in plain vanilla RPA or a more advanced Intelligent Automation. A well set up CoE can select the right processes for automation, and build and deploy the same seamlessly, while delivering the promised benefits, and all of these in collaboration and alignment with the business and IT teams. Let us now discuss the main functions of CoE and how we can set up CoE in an enterprise.

Functions of Automation CoE

In this section, we will discuss what the functions of an Automation CoE are. We have already discussed that to achieve the goals of scaling automation; the CoE broadly provides leadership, guidance, enablement, and governance with respect to automation. For this, the Automation CoE has people, process, technology, and governance as the foundation pillars or dimensions. These dimensions are interrelated and will work in sync to provide this to drive the success in the automation journey. Simply put, what this means is that you need to have the right people enabled, who can select the right processes for automation. There should be a right technology platform with the relevant hardware and software, architecture, and policies. There is a need to have the right kind of governance across the lifecycle.

Before we detail out the four dimensions, let us quickly understand the key stakeholders of an Automation CoE. The primary stakeholders are as follows:

- CoE Sponsor
- CoE Lead, CoE Architect, CoE Process Consultants
- Business Leads from Business Units
- Automation Delivery Team

- Automation Support Team
- IT Infrastructure Team

Now, depending on the structure of the organization, these stake holders may be represented by a single or multiple people in the organization. But what is key to understand is that each of these stakeholders have some responsibility and accountability in the automation lifecycle. They may belong to the IT units or the Business units . Their roles and extent of control and influence in driving automation will be defined by the CoE Operating Model.

The four dimensions mentioned earlier are key in the functioning of a CoE. The primary responsibility of a CoE can be grouped under six categories in the context of automation. The following diagram gives a quick snapshot to those broad activities:

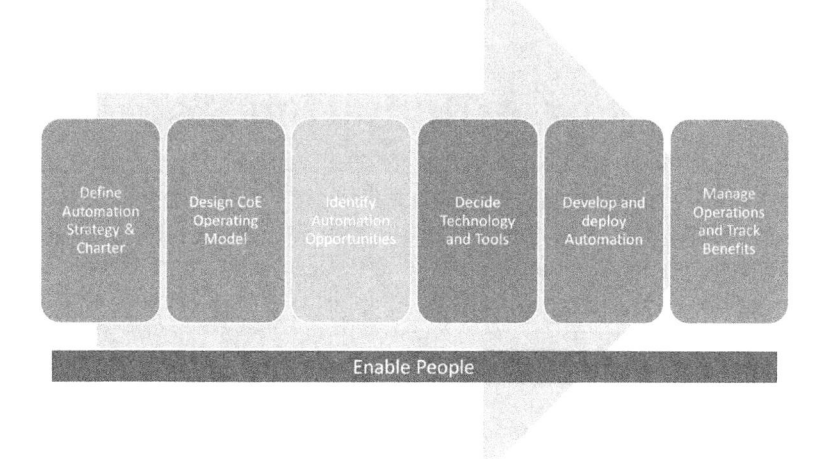

Figure 6.3: *Functions of an Automation Centre of Excellence*

To perform these activities, a CoE needs to build up on the core foundation pillars that we mentioned earlier. Let us now dive deep inot each of these CoE dimensions and see how they relate to the overall functioning of the CoE. Take a look at the following diagram to understand the dimensions of an Automation CoE:

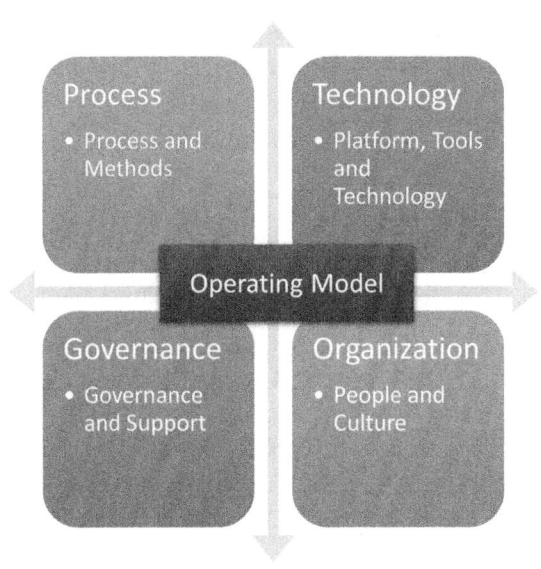

Figure 6.4: Dimensions of an Automation CoE

Organization

A key dimension of the Automation CoE is defining how it will be organized and operated. This is not just defining the organization structure but encompassing a lot more than that. The structure of a CoE will be dependent on its operating model and the operating model of the CoE will depend on the organizational construct and the drivers and objectives. To define the organization of the CoE, we need to think from the basics – start with the vision, mission, objectives, and goals of the CoE. This will clearly lay down the drivers and the desired outcomes of the CoE. Based on these, we will decide on the operating model of the Automation CoE. Let us talk about the various operating models and how to decide which model is right for you.

Different models of CoE

There are a few common operating models when it comes to an Automation CoE. These can be listed as follows:

- **Centralized CoE**: Where the complete control and ownership of automation lies with the CoE, and the business units are more in a consulting role. In this model, CoE is the primary provider of automation in the enterprise.

- **Federated CoE**: Where the business units run their own automation initiatives and have satellite or mini CoEs. The business units are in complete control of the automation and there is no central control and ownership.

- **Hybrid CoE**: This can have various combinations with a mixed mode of control and ownership between the business units and the Automation CoE with varying degrees of ownership to match the priorities of the enterprise.

At this juncture, it is important to understand that the CoE may or may not belong to the core IT organization of the enterprise. It can be a separate entity within the enterprise, a part of the CIO's organization, or the COO's organization, but having a close collaboration with the business units and IT. The positioning of the CoE in the enterprise is one of the important factors to consider while deciding on the operating model.

The question that has probably arisen in your mind by now, is how to decide what kind of operating model we need. For that, we need to understand the pros and cons of each of the operating models and then assess the models for fitment in the context of your enterprise, taking into consideration, the drivers and outcomes expected from the CoE. The following section details out the various models with the pros and cons of each model at a high level.

Centralized CoE Model

A centralized CoE is one in which the control and ownership of automation completely lies with the CoE. In this model, the CoE will support all the business units for all their automation requirements. The CoE will be responsible for identifying the automation opportunities, developing and deploying them. The CoE will also be responsible for all tools and technology decisions, including an automation platform if required. They will also maintain the pool of skilled resources that can deliver the automation for the business.

Since it is centralized and unified, there is good expertise, knowledge sharing, and skill accumulation in the CoE. It is easier to govern and disseminate the best practices within the organization. In many cases, the centralized CoEs are owned by the IT organization and are an extension if it. A centralized CoE is easily scalable and is usually a preferred choice during the phase of the automation journey, when rapid scale is desired, and control and governance are very important.

The disadvantage of such a CoE model is that, since it is completely controlled and managed by a centralized team, the business needs from the different business units might need to be prioritized, which may not match the business unit's expectation or priority. The bandwidth of the CoE may become a bottleneck. There may be a waiting time between the time the automation request is made by the specific business unit and the automation is finally deployed, and hence careful planning and prioritization may be essential for the rapid scaling and matching the expectations of the business.

Federated CoE

A federated or a decentralized CoE, as the name indicates, is somewhat opposite to a centralized one. In this model, the business units have their own smaller CoEs which are responsible for the identification, development, and deployment of the automation. They usually have their own tools and technology platforms and separate pool of resources, owned and managed by themselves, or they can also loan the resources from a central pool, based on how the enterprise is structured. The control of automation in the enterprise is, therefore, distributed between the business units, and there is no central ownership and control. This model may be preferred during the initial phases of automation, when the business units are experimenting with the automation technologies and validating the business benefits. However, as the automation needs to scale, this type of model may not be appropriate. Since there is no central automation platform, the management and maintenance efforts significantly increase, as they are duplicated across the business units. Additionally, there is a lack of effective knowledge management and sharing since the resources belong to different the business units and are not part of a common pool. However, since this model gives the business units complete control over the automation, their individual priorities are very well addressed and managed.

Hybrid Model

As the name indicates, this is a mix of both the centralized and the federated. Here, the CoE will provide the umbrella of leadership, innovation, and governance. This CoE will have a strong participation and stake from the business units and IT. There will be smaller satellite CoEs for the larger business units or geographies which will be managed by the main CoE. There is a good scope of knowledge sharing and resource sharing that can be defined between the main and the mini CoEs. This model can be tailored to suit the enterprise's needs easily with the right mix of participation, ownership, and control from the business and IT teams. The hybrid model also has a multidisciplinary participation from both the business and the IT. The process and opportunity identification are usually driven by the participating business units and the delivery and deployment is managed by the participating IT Units. The hybrid model mitigates the disadvantages of both the centralized and the decentralized models and seems more fit in most automation transformation journeys for the enterprise. However, it may need more planning and cost to set up such a hybrid CoE.

The following figure is a quick snapshot of the different models at a glance:

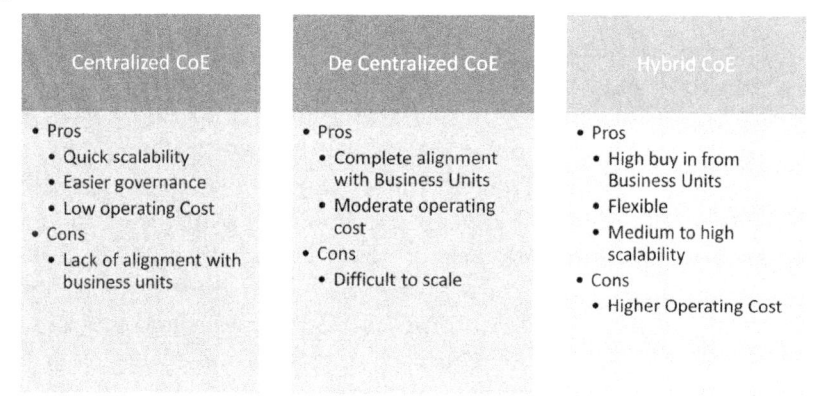

Centralized CoE	De Centralized CoE	Hybrid CoE

• Pros
  • Quick scalability
  • Easier governance
  • Low operating Cost
• Cons
  • Lack of alignment with business units
	• Pros
	  • Complete alignment with Business Units
	  • Moderate operating cost
	• Cons
	  • Difficult to scale
		• Pros
		  • High buy in from Business Units
		  • Flexible
		  • Medium to high scalability
		• Cons
		  • Higher Operating Cost

Figure 6.5: CoE Operating Models at a glance

At this point, what is important to understand is that there no single silver bullet for the automation CoE operating model. Each enterprise has their own drivers, challenges, structure, and culture. All of these play an important role in deciding which CoE model will be the best fit for them. The preceding characteristics of the models provide you the guidance that will help you decide the model in a specific scenario within your enterprise.

The CoE Operating model, thus, defines how the CoE will operate within the enterprise. The stakeholders for each phase in the lifecycle of the automation is decided and the interactions are guided based on the operating model.

Another important aspect in this organization dimension, apart from the CoE operating model, is about the funding and sustenance of the CoE. Typically, in a centralized model, it will be funded by the CIO's organization and will charge back to the business units based on the automation delivered. There could be different arrangements based on the effort or benefits or the other factors as relevant in the enterprise. In case of a federated or decentralized model, the business units will typically own and fund the CoEs and consume the benefits it generates. In case of hybrid, where there is a strong participation and the stakes are high from the business units, IT teams, and the CoE, there needs to be a strong benefit measurement framework to enable the CoE to charge back to the various business units, based on their levels of participation in the CoE, and also payback the IT in case CoE is consuming any of their services like Infrastructure hosting and management.

Let us now touch upon the people enablement activity that is key for a CoE to grow, scale, and deliver. The CoE is responsible for creating awareness about automation within the enterprise. It needs to conduct formal and informal education and awareness sessions, so that people can appreciate the power of automation, start ideating about the automation opportunities, that will add value to them and their customers, and ease out the resistance to automation adoption. In terms of building the skills around automation, the CoE should lay down the training and learning plans for the different roles and levels of skills for the business and technical resources. They can impart such education themselves or partner with the internal and external Learning Management Services to do that for them. With efficient monitoring, tracking, and validating through external and internal certifications, the training and learning plans can help to create a steady pipeline of resources for automation.

The other impact is how to manage the re-organization due to automation. The key drivers of automation are cost reduction, efficiency improvement and FTE savings. But as the FTEs are released from a particular process that has been automated, how do we reskill and redeploy the resource, needs to be thought of as a strategy while we are defining the overall automation strategy? Hence, an especially important aspect of the CoE is change management. How to manage the organizational, operational, and governance changes that result from automation need to be given a deep thought to develop a change management strategy that will outline how the automated operations will look like, and how to redeploy the resources that are freed after the successful automation. Making the Change Management Strategy transparent for all the stakeholders can add a lot of value and increase the automation adoption in the long run.

Lastly, before we go to the other important dimensions, let us discuss what kind of structure and staffing should a CoE typically have. In *figure 6.6*, we have listed down some of the core roles and how they roll up to the CoE leadership. This is an indicative structure to provide you with a guideline and initial construct. You can start with a lean CoE which could be a subset of this structure if it seems fit or start with a similar structure and tailor it according to the specific needs of automation and their organization structure in the enterprise. Take a look at the following diagram to understand the CoE organization structure:

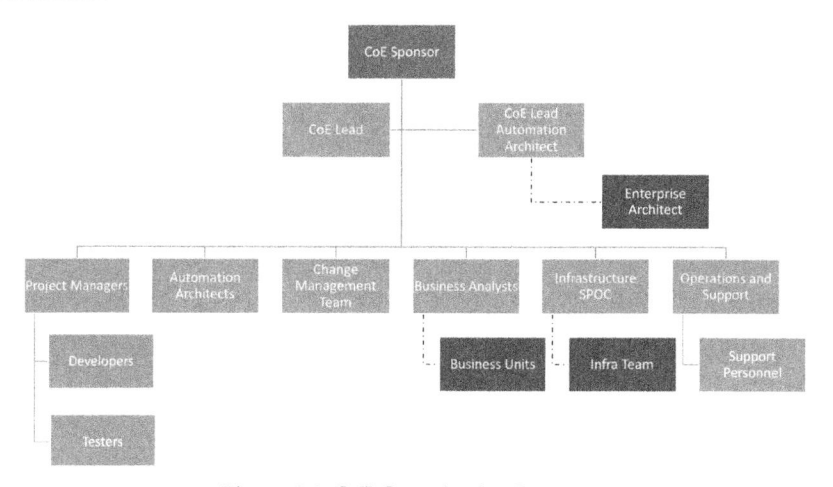

Figure 6.6: CoE Organization Structure

As you can see in the preceding diagram, the CoE is a multi-disciplinary team with each member bringing in his or her expertise to achieve the overall success of automation in the enterprise.

Process

This dimension includes defining the process, methods, and frameworks for the automation lifecycle. Right from defining the method for identifying the process to be automated, to the delivery framework and support model for managing and monitoring the automation, this dimension covers it all. Hence, this dimension includes the definition of the opportunity identification method, design and development method, and the support framework. While setting up the CoE, these methods need to be defined and elaborated, as well as be aligned to the enterprise-wide design, delivery, and support processes. The tasks and activities involved in each method should be described and an estimation model should be provided for each so that when the CoE is operational, these artifacts provide a definite structure and aid in the automation delivery lifecycle. In the following section, let us discuss a few important considerations that should be included when defining these methods.

Opportunity Identification Method: While defining the method for identifying the processes, we need to keep in mind the technical and non-technical characteristics of the processes that we discussed in detail in *Chapter 2:Robotic Process Automation, Chapter 3: Artificial Intelligence and Chapter 4 : Other Automation Technologies.*. It would be good to create a weighted model based on these characteristics to arrive at an objective criterion for the process identification. The inputs to the model will be the technical and non-technical characteristics of the processes and the output should be an indication of how good a fit the process is for the automation. Many automation product vendors and automation service provides provide such process selection models for the evaluation of the processes for automation. You could look at some of these that are available freely over the internet to get an idea and create a model of your own that will suit your requirements for your enterprise. As the recent trends show, the latest toolset in identifying the automation opportunities is coming out in the form of the process and task mining tools. We will touch upon Process Mining in the final chapter of this book.

The design and delivery methods should also be defined in this dimension of CoE. It would be prudent to create a design and delivery method in line with the enterprise design and delivery framework while adding in the specific automation activities and tasks as required. There should be checkpoints or validation gates as the automation moves from requirements, design, delivery, test, and so on. Based on the requirements and enterprise delivery models, the methodology could be agile or waterfall, based on the need and fitment. However, agile may be better applicable as automation is a new technological experience in the enterprise and might need frequent loopbacks between the stakeholders.

One of the important methods defined by the CoE, in addition to design and delivery, is the support mechanism. It is particularly important to define the different levels (Levels 1, 2, and 3) of support and clearly demonstrate how the support mechanism will work, once a bot or automata or the other automation component fails in production. In matured organizations, which have scaled significantly, it might make sense to lay down a structure with the tools and technology on how to automate some of these levels of support. If a situation arises where, to manage and maintain the bots and other automation, you need a significant pool of resources, it kind of defeats the cost driver of automation. So, as an enterprise scales automation, it is important to start thinking of automating the support structure. While defining the CoE, it is a good juncture to define such a framework and the roadmap to achieve the same.

We have seen that, based on the vision, mission, objectives, and outcome, an automation roadmap is created as part of the Automation Strategy, while setting up the CoE in the organization dimension. This roadmap as well as the operating model, along with the organization's existing processes that has worked well in relevant areas should be the key inputs, as we are defining the process identification, delivery, and support methodologies for the CoE.

The process dimension also takes care of the various tools, templates, and artifacts that are necessary to deliver the automation at scale. As part of the CoE set up, an integrated tool chain can be recommended to cover the tooling around the automation lifecycle. The tool chain needs to be extended beyond the process dimension to include the organization, technology, and governance to provide an end-to-end view of the automation in a dashboard. It might take time and cost to set up such an integrated tool chain, but it will eventually add a lot of value and clarity to the automation journey.

The following diagram summarizes the process dimension responsibilities:

Process
- Process Identification method
- Automation Delivery method
- Support method

Tools
- Templates, Frameworks
- Integrated ToolChain

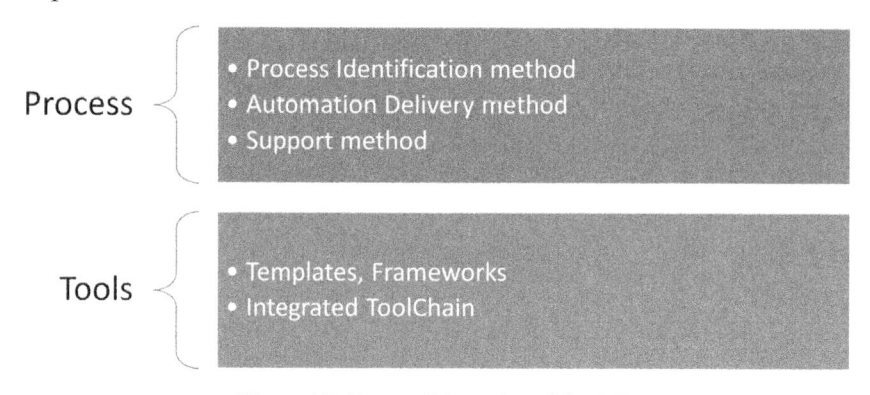

Figure 6.7: *Process Dimension of the CoE*

Technology

The automation CoE also plays an especially important role around the automation technology. Making the appropriate decisions about the technologies and products are particularly important in the automation journey. The primary function of the technology dimension is to define and decide the right automation tools, products and frameworks for the enterprise. This is not a one-off decision and involves defining an enterprise architecture for automation, which considers how automation will fit into the existing ecosystem and thrive. One of the key expectations from a CoE in the technology dimension is thus, to define the Enterprise Automation Architecture and the associated technology, products, tools, and solutions for the automation lifecycle. The implementation of the Automation enterprise architecture plus the tool chain will result in an Automation Platform for the enterprise. As you can see, this is one of the areas, where the technology and process dimensions of CoE are working together. Defining the Automation Enterprise Architecture and a Platform might sound like a heavy monolithic structure, but in reality, it needs to be a seamless aggregation and integration with several tools, technologies, and frameworks to build the capability and host the services that will have interoperability, and will make Intelligent Automation in an enterprise feasible.

As part of the technology track, defining the automation reference architecture is a key prerequisite that will help an enterprise make the Automation Platform real. To explain in simple terms, the automation reference architecture is the blueprint, which when mapped to the specific tools, products, and solutions, become the Enterprise Automation Architecture. As we implement these products and tools and make them real, hosted on the enterprise hardware, we call it the Automation Platform. All these three together with the timelines and priority, will help us define the Automation Technology Roadmap.

The reference architecture is thus made up of the technical building blocks that will be necessary to implement the automation vision of the enterprise. In many engagements that I have worked on, these are a set of blueprints – the first one is the reference architecture identifying all the building block matching the automation vision and requirements of the enterprise, and the second one is a more detailed one with a phased approach and recommended tools/products that evolve into the Enterprise Automation Architecture. Through this phased approach, we can define how to traverse through the various stages of automation while being completely aligned and driven by the business outcomes and build the Automation Platform. The technology dimension of the CoE is thus, responsible to define when to embrace what technology, based on the business needs. The technology dimension would answer the questions on how to move from the simple RPA and assisted automation to the chatbots and how to bring in more advanced technologies like the machine learning or blockchain. A phased approach to develop the various building blocks with their implementation decision and recommended solutions needs to be created as part of the technology dimension that will eventually evolve into an Automation Technology roadmap and then evolve into the Automation Platform for the enterprise.

Another important aspect that the technology dimension handles is the scalability, availability, performance, and the other non-functional requirements of automation. These should also be handled with the Enterprise Automation Architecture definition. The architecture should define the hosting of the different components and building blocks, integration mechanisms, security policies etc., while defining the technology blueprint.

The Automation Technology Roadmap of the CoE, thus, reflects and defines this complete enterprise architecture and the phased approach to realize the automation building blocks. In later steps, each building block is mapped to different technical components which can be custom built or bought off the shelf products and tools. The build vs buy decision for these components and a high-level implementation roadmap is also an important decision taken by the Automation CoE. The roadmap therefore, is now aligned to the automation vision of the enterprise and is key in laying down the foundation of a successful automation journey of the enterprise and the underlying Automation Platform.

The technology dimension also lays down the architectural principles and guidelines for automation. The principles around reusability, flexibility, and extensibility of the design should be thought about carefully, since these lay important foundation from the design perspective as the automation scales. Conducting the proof of concept or proof of technology for the new technologies are some of the other activities of the technology dimension.

There is co-ownership of this dimension with the process dimension, to ensure that the design and delivery frameworks are correctly adhered to and that the different automation solutions that are built/

bought, adhere to the automation principles and policies laid down by this dimension of the CoE.

Governance

Governance is a key dimension when it comes to the Intelligent Automation CoE. The CoE must provide the overarching umbrella of governance to the entire automation lifecycle. As part of the governance, the various governance bodies, necessary for the automation lifecycle, is defined and their interactions are outlined. The various governance meetings, their participants, frequencies, and expectations are also outlined in this dimension to streamline the interactions.

The governance dimension also outlines the mechanism for the benefit measurement and tracking to assess the progress against the established automation strategy. For this, the CoE needs to define the KPIs that will measure the success of the automation deployed and identify a method to measure and report the same and work along with the process and technology dimensions on defining the tools to track and manage the benefits. So, from a governance perspective, there needs to be a few KPIs defined for the CoE as a whole. This could be in terms of the number of automation deployed, the number of FTE redeployed, the automation delivery rate, speed to value etc. While defining the operating model, these KPIs can be decided, and later, as the CoE becomes operational, these need to be measured and reported. Another key area for Governance is to create a detailed RACI matrix – defining the role of the different stakeholders in each of the different activities in the lifecycle of an automation project.

Now that we have covered all the four dimensions, we will discuss a few points that are to be noted while setting up and implementing a CoE. Usually, in the initial days of automation, the primary technology may be RPA. However, while setting up a CoE, we need to keep in mind that we are setting it up for Intelligent Automation, and so, we should not contain the scope to RPA only, even though that may be the ongoing automation at that time. So, while defining the operating model, the design and delivery framework, and the support and governance models, we need to think from a broader perspective, keeping in mind the overall automation strategy and the different automation technologies that will have a key role in the overall success of automation.

The second point to note is that the IT and the business are equal partners and both are particularly important in a successful CoE operation. The CoE can belong to either the CIO's organization or a COO's organization, but a close collaboration, trust, and partnership needs to be built and nurtured continuously.

Setting Up a CoE

Setting up a CoE needs a lot of understanding of the organization and the drivers of automation for an enterprise. This should be done by a dedicated team of automation SMEs, architects, and CoE specialists, in collaboration with the IT and Business Leads. This should be managed as a project as opposed to the people working voluntarily and creating methods and processes. Many organizations hire external consultants from the consulting firms to help them design the CoE operating model and set up the CoE.

Now that we have discussed and understood how a CoE is organized and how it functions, let us touch upon some of the points which are important for a CoE to be successful.

First and foremost is the executive sponsorship and backing for the CoE along with a well-defined vision and automation strategy. In the absence of either of these, the Automation CoE or the automation journey can fall flat.

The second most important item is to define the operating model, since that will define the entire ecosystem within the automation organization. A well thought out operating model can make the automation journey seamless, with each stakeholder's priorities and expectations being taken care of. The rest of the things like the enterprise architecture, delivery frameworks, governance models, enablement, and change management can all be covered if the operating model is well defined.

Conclusion

In this chapter, we discussed the enterprise automation journey and the importance of having an Automation CoE in the enterprise's automation journey. We understood the challenges that most enterprises are facing today in scaling automation and also discussed how setting up an Automation CoE is extremely critical for the overall success of automation in an enterprise in the face of these challenges.

Setting up and operating a CoE needs resources and funds, but they play a key role in making the automation successful. It not only helps to develop and manage the automation opportunities seamlessly but also plays a key role in the enablement and adoption of automation in the enterprise. We discussed that when setting up the CoE for Intelligent Automation, it is advisable to include the multidisciplinary teams, participating from the various technology and business teams to bring in their perspective of automation and how the different dimensions of CoE, staffed by these multidisciplinary teams work in sync, first to define, and then to operate the CoE, enabling the enterprise to deliver a successful automation.

So far in this book, we have discussed the automation technologies, Automation CoE, automation roadmap and implementation, and the real use cases and their solutions. With those knowledge, you are almost ready to go and take on the world with your Intelligent Automation ideas and practices.

In the final chapter, let us discuss a few important topics about the latest trends and things that are still evolving and how the future of work is shaping up amidst the pandemic related turmoil in the society and industry.

Further Reading

- https://www.gartner.com/en/documents/3872494/how-to-scale-rpa-and-achieve-business-value-in-utilities
- https://www.gartner.com/en/documents/3980208/scale-automation-in-healthcare-using-a-center-of-excelle
- https://www.gartner.com/en/documents/3985957/customer-experience-driven-automation-implementation-gui
- https://searchcio.techtarget.com/feature/Why-CIOs-need-to-establish-an-automation-CoE

Chapter 7
Intelligent Automation – Trends and the Future

Introduction

By now, we have a good grip on Intelligent Automation. In the journey from the start of this book to here, we have covered the definition of Intelligent Automation, discussed in detail the technologies, understood how to build automation and scale it across the enterprise, and finally discussed several important use cases and their technical solutions.

In this final chapter of this book, we will discuss some of the newer things that are happening in this area and being talked about in the context of Intelligent Automation. There are interesting topics like how process mining can be leveraged in Intelligent Automation, what does citizen development in RPA mean, how is AI applied in IT Operations or AIOps, and so on. These are some of the key topics that are trending in the Intelligent Automation space and are coming up in most CIO discussions across the board. There are many reports and papers around these topics by analysts like Forrester, Gartner, HFS, and so on. We will discuss these topics in this chapter to brief you about the latest. The final topic that we will cover in this book is the Future of Work. We have addressed the concept of the future of work briefly in *Chapter 1, Introduction to Automation*. Now that we have traversed the entire lifecycle of Intelligent Automation, it makes perfect sense to delve a little deeper into this topic and understand the impacts of Intelligent Automation in our work, in the businesses, and in our society.

Today, we see a strong shift towards digitization and digital transformation. Businesses across the enterprises already have the focus on digital transformation, and automation was always a key enabler. Covid-19 simply accelerated this shift and made it more important. There is now a bigger push to adopt and scale automation and that goes beyond the RPA automation and extends into the Intelligent Automation with AI. This is now not limited to the back-office business processes or shared service operations. There is a strong eagerness to extend this across the enterprise and scale.

Structure

In this chapter, we will discuss the following topic:

- **Process Mining**: Basic concepts and how it works.
- **Citizen Development**: Why is it gaining importance in the enterprises in the context of Intelligent Automation?
- **AIOps**: How AI Led IT Operations plans to transform the operations landscape.
- **Future of Work**: How Intelligent Automation is impacting it and how can enterprises gear up for the change.

Objective

After reading this chapter, you will be able to appreciate and talk about the latest trends in Intelligent Automation around Process Mining, the leading tools in the space, and why we should leverage Process Mining in the context of Intelligent Automation. You will be able to understand and articulate the pros and cons of citizen development with respect to automation. You will also be able to understand and assess the fitment of AIOps in the IT operations and create a roadmap to implement AIOps in an enterprise. You will be able to appreciate the concept of the future of work and understand the need for a shift in the culture and operating model of the organization, as more and more processes get automated and a hybrid workforce work in a seamless transition.

Process Mining

Process Mining has become an important topic in most CIO conversations today. This is because, as we strive towards making the processes more efficient, the first thing we need to focus on, is to assess the current processes, find out if they are working as defined, what the areas of inefficiencies are that has creeped in, and/or whether the process is obsolete and needs a complete make over. These assessments are not only required with respect to automation but are needed for process engineering and lean initiatives as well. In the context of Intelligent Automation, we discussed how to automate the business and IT processes, how to identify which processes to be automated, and then how to take them forward for the automation delivery and manage and monitor the benefits of automation. In this lifecycle, there is a strong tendency to apply automation as a lever, to resolve any kind of process inefficiencies. Whenever there is a need to improve the performance of a process, we tend to first identify the areas that can be automated, without applying much thought to the state of the process itself. In many cases, that automation lever may be the best fit and the right thing to do to improve the efficiency. However, there can be cases, where the process itself needs a relook. Automating an inefficient process will result in an inefficient process automation, without the core problem getting resolved. Process mining plays a key role in this area in the context of Intelligent Automation to identify the inefficiencies and provide the data driven discovery to identify the root cause of the inefficiencies.

Process Mining is thus, a data driven discovery of the various activities and tasks in a process and uncovering the relevant insights (based on the data and meta data) about their performance, variations, non-conformances and others. . It makes the processes and the underlying activities visible end to end at a great detail, to identify the issues in an operation based on the data from the running processes. It can be understood as a combination of data mining and process analytics to uncover the hidden issues or problems and reveal the areas of improvement.

Process Mining can be leveraged with different goals in mind. It can be used to validate if the processes are conforming to the documented business process in the enterprise. It can be used to identify the variations, repetitions, and bottlenecks in the process that may not be very apparent otherwise. Being data driven, it helps us to understand exactly what is happening throughout the lifecycle of the process at every activity and capture objective information about them. For process mining to work, we need real operational data about the operating process from the run time environment. This includes data from and around the event logs from the systems that are executing the processes. Typically, the ERP systems, CRM systems, etc., provide an audit trail and event logs along with the associated data out of the box. This data is ingested in process mining to create the visual representation of the flow of activities that are executed or a process graph. The pictorial visualization of the process flow and its variations, enables the process owners and process analysts to see how the process is functioning, whether there is any necessity for process optimization or process redesigning, and where automation can be leveraged. Apart from the visual representation, process mining can generate insights on the performance of the process and the various activities. The insights generated from process mining serve as the inputs to identifying the opportunities for automation. However, one of the issues with using process mining across all kinds of processes could be the availability of the relevant data. Since it needs the event logs as the input, the manual activities or activities through the productivity tools like Word, Excel, or Citrix based applications, that do not generate event logs, may not be automatically discovered by process mining. However, the tools available in the market are continuously evolving and matching the requirements of the market to address such issues

Take a look at the following diagram to understand Process Mining:

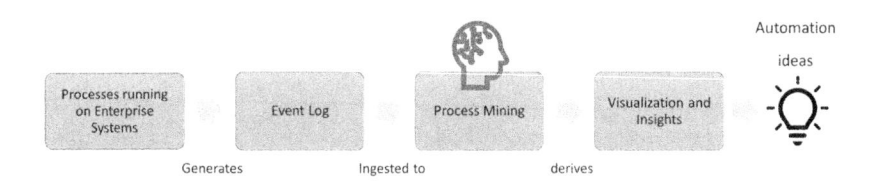

Figure 7.1: Process Mining

Now that we have a fair idea about what process mining is, from the preceding diagram, let us try to understand how process mining can be leveraged in Intelligent Automation.

Importance of process mining in the context of Intelligent Automation

Process mining can be a powerful tool in the context of automation. Most enterprises today, identify the processes for automation based on the process analysis done by SMEs. We have discussed this type of analysis in *Chapter 2, Robotic Process Automation* and *Chapter 3, Artificial Intelligence* in detail. Primarily, the criteria like repeatability, rule-based process, structured or unstructured data, play an important role in determining if a process is fit for automation and what would be the primary lever of automation. This approach works well; however, it needs human intelligence and a talented resource pool to scale. With process mining, a significant part of this analysis can be automatically analyzed by the Process Mining tools. This analysis, therefore, would be completely data driven and would be beneficial in identifying the processes for automation in an automated way. This would also help to take some of the load off the human analysts and enable them to focus on the interpretation of the insights generated by the process mining tools to identify the right processes and their relevant levers of automation.

It is a common fact, that a bulk of use cases which are identified for automation, are usually from the various back office and mid office systems like an **Enterprise Resource Planning (ERP)** or a **Customer Management System (CRM)**, and so on. For these types of processes, the event logs and activity logs are available out of the box with most enterprise systems. Process mining brings out remarkably interesting data and insights in these cases, that can be leveraged to understand the specific drawbacks of the process. The insights on which activities in a process are continuously repeated, which activities are of extremely high volume, and even the user productivity data and cycle times of the activity and tasks can be leveraged to identify the techniques to make the process better. These data collectively can be used to model the automation potential of the process objectively and even quantify the benefits that the automation can bring in.

In this context, there is another aspect related to process mining, which is gaining a lot of traction and that is task mining. Task mining is the mining of the data related to the UI level interaction of the users with the system. While process mining tells you how the process is performing, task mining gives you insights on how efficiently or inefficiently the users are interacting with the system.

Manual activities like filling in a form, copying the data to and from a spreadsheet, writing a report on a word processor like MS Word, and so on, can be detected and mined through task mining. Through task mining, the manual activities and their meta data can be captured effectively. The analysis of the processes through task mining tools mean that relevant clickstream data must be collected and fed to the tool to derive the insights.

Combining process mining with task mining gives a holistic view of the process, on how it is being used by a user in the context of the business. With process mining and task mining combined, we get a visual representation of the process graph, with potential problematic areas based on volume, accuracy, repeatability, efficiency, highlighted. These can help us determine the process changes or improvements that are needed and how automation can solve them. In addition, some process mining tools also have the capability to simulate the *"what if"* scenarios, that can further help validate the relevance of automation as the process improvement lever.

Let us now touch upon the specific benefits and advantages of Process Mining. As already mentioned, process mining is applicable in many areas beyond automation. In fact, applying the process and task mining for automation is just one of the many ways that we can apply the insights derived from process mining.

The output of process mining can be directed towards three primary objectives. They are as follows:

- Discovering the end to end process based on the event data.
- Validating whether the process is executed in conformance to the way it should be.
- Identifying any areas of improvement.

So, the primary value addition of process mining is identifying the inefficiencies and non-conformances. These can be taken as the inputs to process reengineering or process enhancement initiatives to influence the increase in efficiency and cost reduction through the appropriate enterprise initiatives.

There are several process mining tools in the market, ranging from having the basic capabilities of generating the process graph to the complex and advanced analysis of process using AI. Many Process Mining tools combine the power of AI to group the activities, map them to the business KPIs, and generate insights on how to optimize the processes both from a process design and a user management perspective. This holistic analysis has become valuable and is adding a lot of value to the identification of the processes for automation. Take a look at the following diagram to understand the converged approach of combining Process and Task Mining:

```
[Process Mining] + [Task Mining] → [Insights on Process and User Performance / Suggested Automation if any]
```

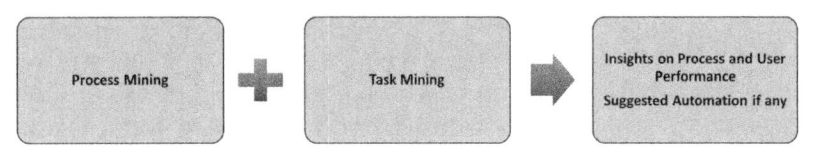

Figure 7.2: *Converged Approach – Process and Task Mining*

As you can see in the preceding diagram, this converged approach helps to identify a lot of key parameters, like which activities are manual, which activities are taking longer time, the user performance against any enterprise benchmark, the KPI comparison against benchmarks, and the others at different levels of granularity. These data can be very effective to assess the current state of the process, both from the way the process is performing, and the way users are operating and executing the process. The identification of the areas of automation and insights around the primary levers of automation can be determined based on such analysis. In the context of Intelligent Automation, a combination of process and task mining can be used to conduct a detailed analysis of a process identified, to quantify the automation potential, specify areas of automation, and project the precise data driven benefit numbers.

However, it should be kept in mind that process mining is no silver bullet. If you procure a process mining tool, and analyze the processes through it, an opportunity pipeline of the identified processes will not be generated automatically. You need to follow the structured way of analyzing and qualifying a process for Intelligent Automation as described in chapter *Chapter 2: Robotic Process Automation, Chapter 3: Artificial Intelligence and* and *Chapter 4: Other Technologies for Automation*. You should embed process mining as a supplementary tool while conducting a detailed analysis of the processes that have been shortlisted based on the high-level business value projected. The tool should be an enabler to your qualifying process and not the other way round. Through this, you would be able to plan and leverage the process mining usage for the best outcome possible.

Leveraging process mining in an enterprise would mean, you would need to procure the licenses for such a tool – either on premise or as a service offering. It would mean evaluating the various process mining tools that would fit the requirements of usage, procuring the licenses for the tool, building the capability, and having trained resources to use the tool for process analysis. The resources can be insourced or outsourced depending on the capability and operating model of the enterprise.

Another important point in the context of process mining is, process mining should always be done with an objective in mind, outlining why we want to do process mining, and how we are going to apply the insights generated. Since there can be various ways to leverage process mining, defining the objective upfront will help to do the right type of analysis and drive towards realizing the goals of process mining better. Thus, a well thought out and planned approach to leverage process mining in the context of Intelligent Automation is essential to truly utilizing the power of process mining that can be of essential value to the enterprises in their Automation journey.

By now, you have an idea about the process mining, its capabilities, and where it can be used with respect to Intelligent Automation. Let us end this discussion with a list of some of the market leading Process Mining tools.

In the recent times, there has been a lot of development in the process mining space. New products, niche players, and niche capabilities have arrived, and various players are trying to establish themselves in the market. Many enterprises are starting to conduct proof of concepts and pilots, before finalizing a specific tool as their enterprise process mining tool of choice, based on the objectives of the enterprise. The European enterprises are leading this trend; however, it is visible across North America and Asia Pacific as well. The enterprises are starting mostly with the back-office processes of procurement, finance, and accounting as the launchpads for process mining. The following table (*table 7.1*) lists a few of the market leading tools and platforms available in the market at the time of writing this book.

List of Prominent Process Mining Tools

The following table contains a list of some of the key players (not an exhaustive list in any way) in the market and there are a lot more who are vying to establish themselves. You can look at the websites for more information on their capabilities, solutions, and the kind of enterprise clients they are engaged with, as follows:

Serial No	Process Mining Product/ Platform	Platform Provider URL
1	ABBYY Timeline	https://www.abbyy.com/timeline/discovering-and-mapping/
2	Celonis	https://www.celonis.com/
3	FortressIQ	https://www.fortressiq.com/solution/process-intelligence/
4	Kryon	https://www.kryonsystems.com/process-discovery/
5	Minit	https://www.minit.io/process-simulation
6	MyInvenio	https://www.my-invenio.com/
7	NICE	https://www.nice.com/
8	Signavio	https://www.signavio.com/process-mining/
9	SoftwareAG ARIS	https://www.softwareag.com/en_corporate/platform/aris/process-mining.html
10	UiPath Process Gold	https://www.uipath.com/product/process-mining

Table 7.1: List of Process Mining tools

Citizen Development

Citizen development is a practice in which the business users with little coding and software development experience are building applications in their enterprise environments. According to Gartner as stated in the Gartner Glossary, *"A citizen developer is a user who creates new business applications for consumption by others using development and runtime environments sanctioned by corporate IT."* What is important to note in this definition is that the citizen developer's role is different from that of an enterprise developer. With the rise in demand to build various small and medium enterprise apps catering to the various types of users' needs, the depth of the business knowledge residing with the business users, and the availability of the low-code platforms for development, Citizen Development is a trend that is on the rise.

Rising Trend of Citizen Development

Citizen Development is opening a lot of opportunities for the whole enterprise, and especially in automation. The enterprise automation resources with the right skills, like the various RPA tools are getting scarce. The business users are becoming tech-savvy and tend to use external, enterprise-unapproved tools to get their job done. In such a situation, any automation that they may develop for personal, or group usage will directly impact their top-line positively and add value to their job role. This shift is leading to a democratization of the development of applications in the enterprise and is getting accelerated with the availability of the low-code no-code platforms.

As the enterprises are moving towards digital transformation, which got accelerated due to the Covid-19 pandemic, there is a huge backlog of IT applications in most enterprises. These may be the small scale applications, automating the parts of the jobs done by specific roles, but nevertheless, important and essential to a different group of employees. Hence, the IT teams are under significant pressure to deliver these applications to the relevant users to meet their goals of digital transformation.

The business users who are doing repetitive mundane jobs are also eager to change their employee experience with all the new technology that is coming into the enterprise. There is frustration among some of these tech savvy new generation business users who really want to leverage the power of technology without being dependent on the Enterprise IT. These users, when enabled, can leverage their business domain expertise to build the applications to automate the activities that they do themselves and/or their workgroups.

From the enterprise standpoint, due to the significant IT backlogs, there are situations of missed targets, and missed cost reduction opportunities. Citizen Development opens up an avenue to broaden their developer pool, along with an opportunity to address the employee experience, both for the business users and the IT resources. So, to the enterprises, Citizen Development is a concept which almost poses a win-win opportunity, and they are interested in leveraging it to the fullest.

In the context of Intelligent Automation, it's more so. Process automation is tremendously dependent on the knowledge of the process. Unless the process details are rightfully captured, the automation will not succeed. The business users are the ones who have the best knowledge about the processes; they are also the ones who will gain the maximum benefits and for whom the automation is being built. So it's in their interest, if they can build the automation by themselves and improve the business KPIs like accuracy, cycle time, and so on. Citizen development for them is enabling them to help themselves. In the following diagram (*figure 7.3*), you can see some of the benefits and pitfalls of Citizen Development enumerated; we will discuss this in detail in the following section:

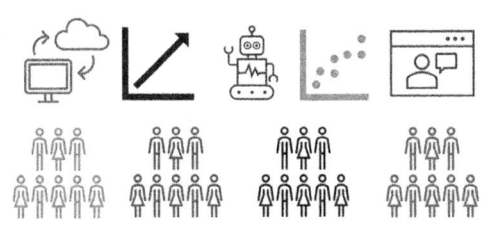

Citizen Development

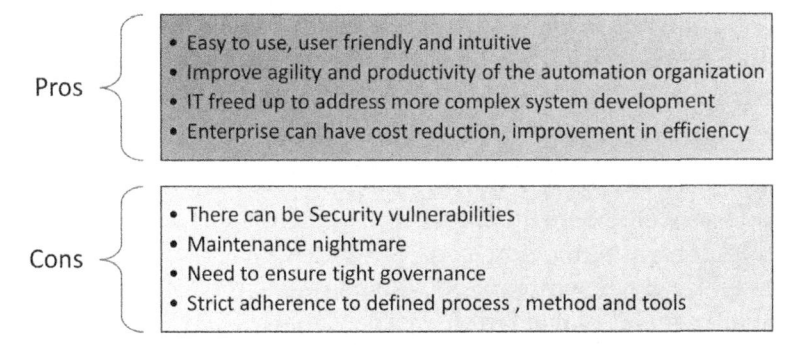

Pros
- Easy to use, user friendly and intuitive
- Improve agility and productivity of the automation organization
- IT freed up to address more complex system development
- Enterprise can have cost reduction, improvement in efficiency

Cons
- There can be Security vulnerabilities
- Maintenance nightmare
- Need to ensure tight governance
- Strict adherence to defined process, method and tools

Figure 7.3: *Citizen Development*

Citizen Development, therefore calls for empowering the business users with the right set of tools, technology, and method to enable them to build the business applications for themselves, for their workgroups, and so on.

However, just like any other good thing, there is always two sides to a coin. Citizen Development comes with its own advantages, as shown in *figure 7.3*, but if not executed and governed within the right framework, it can cause more harm than good to an enterprise.

Citizen Development Platforms in Intelligent Automation

We have seen that citizen development is gaining popularity when it comes to developing the automation solutions in the preceding sections. Let's try to understand how we can enable citizen development in Automation. Are there any requirements from a tool/platform perspective that can help enable the business users faster and allow them to better their employee experience?

First, there should be a evaluation to select the right kind of citizen development tool and platform. There should be a user friendly and intuitive integrated development environment through which the business users can create their automation applications. There needs to be good capabilities, preferably **User Interface (UI)** driven (like drag and drop), to create the process flows, activities, validations, insert business logic in natural language, create user interface, and so on, in a short amount of time and by writing minimum code. There should be some capabilities to debug and figure out problems and automatic testing. Finally, there should be an easy option to deploy the application to the appropriate environment with minimum fuss. From a framework perspective, such a low-code platform should encourage reusability and provide a mechanism to connect to an enterprise automation code library. It should be agile enough to enable the short sprints and collaborative development.

Today, we see a lot of vendors providing such low-code platforms and no-code services to enable the Citizen developers. The rise in Citizen development and the low-code no-code platform in automation today looks like a symbiotic relationship. Each is feeding the other. There are several players in the market, many from the RPA and AI world, who offer an advanced, intuitive development environment which can minimize the amount of code that needs to be written to automate a process.

The citizen development in the Intelligent Automation space is banking a lot upon the low-code no-code platforms. These platforms are typically easy to use and do not need the users to have a deep technical knowledge about software development or the programming language. These are mostly Integrated development environments that are intuitive and user friendly. These are exactly what the tech savvy business users need to build their own automation.

Several RPA vendors have now come up with their citizen development platforms to facilitate such a democratization of bot development. The leading RPA players like UiPath, Automation Anywhere, Microsoft Power Automate and others have built good platforms keeping citizen development in mind. They provide inbuilt security and integration capabilities that can be leveraged by the users easily while adhering to the enterprise technology policies. Various AI platforms like Azure AI, IBM Watson, Google AI services, and many others provide auto machine learning services where you can simply ingest the relevant data, and identify the inputs and output labels, and the platform will automatically create an ML model. The good thing is that such platforms not only provide capabilities for citizen development but also provide more advanced and complex capabilities for the enterprise developers, who are focused on the more complex process automation. Hence, you can have an automation platform with tools and technologies fit for both the citizen and enterprise developers in a harmony. The vendors named earlier are just a few indicative names and there are a lot of other players in the market providing a host of tools and platforms.

In this context, we would like to help you understand an important point. Despite all the marketing and product publicities, it is important to understand that not all low-code is RPA and not all RPA is low-code. While planning for citizen development in the enterprise, there needs to be a careful evaluation of the automation tools, maturity assessment of the automation ecosystem, readiness of the governance framework to handle the diverse challenges and pitfalls of enterprise, and citizen development to have these aspects addressed, and only then can the democratization of automation development thrive.

Pitfalls of Citizen Development

A successful citizen development initiative would need a lot of understanding about the pitfalls of citizen development and adequate mitigation plans for it. Some of the pitfalls of citizen development were depicted earlier in *figure 7.3*. Let's elaborate them here.

Citizen developers are not skilled coders. They need training and development on the key aspects of software development. Based on their business domain knowledge, the functional requirements of the applications will come very easily to them. However, they need to be aware of the non-functional requirements like security, performance, regulatory compliance, authetication and availability . They should be enabled to address these in their application development and the platform or tool should also provide easy features to include the capabilities like authentication and authorization, audit and logs, easy deployment configuration options. Otherwise, citizen development may give rise to vulnerable applications in an enterprise.

Citizen development can give rise to a lot of orphan applications, which may have been created following the nonstandard practices.

This will give rise to a maintenance nightmare. The citizen developers need to be enabled within an enterprise framework to build their apps. This means, there should be well-defined process, method, and tools that they need to adhere to. There should also be a strong governance mechanism that should govern the development, right from the opportunity creation to the deployment for citizen development, just as it is done for the enterprise development. There must be certain controls and validation checks to ensure that the application is fit for enterprise deployment. The updates and changes to the applications also need to have a change management governance structure around them. These can be less rigorous than what we implement in the Enterprise IT, but should be there in place nonetheless.

With a well governed and managed citizen development initiative along with Enterprise IT, the enterprise will be able to derive positive ROI with a mechanism to combine and balance both the approaches. In this context, an Automation CoE, that we discussed in the previous chapter, might be the right place to formulate and enforce such governance in the automation development. The digital transformation strategy and automation strategy owned by the CoE, will be a good place to define the vision and roadmap of such an initiative.

Let us end this topic, with a few of the market leading low-code no-code platforms focused on the RPA automation and regular application development. This is an indicative list, but at the time of writing this book, these were some of the major players.

List of Tools

The following table contains a list of the few leading RPA tools that are gaining market share with regard to Citizen Development in RPA based automation:

Serial No	Platform/Tool	URL
1	UiPath Studio X	https://www.uipath.com/product/studiox
2	Microsoft Power Automate	https://flow.microsoft.com/en-us/
3	Automation Anywhere	https://www.automationanywhere.com/products/aari
4	BluePrism	https://www.blueprism.com/

Table 7.2: Top RPA Platforms for Citizen development

AIOps

AIOps is another trending topic today in the world of automation. AIOps refers to the concept of applying **Artificial Intelligence (AI)** to the IT operations. IT Operations is often a repetitive and labor-intensive function which involves continuous eyeballing of the events, alerts, and errors in the system, and the subsequent resolution. In addition to these, are the errors reported by the various users due to the non-functioning or malfunctioning of the IT systems. Let us first understand the challenges we have in IT operations, as follows:

- With the exponential growth in the data and applications on premise and on cloud in most enterprises, there are a multitude of applications and infrastructure that need constant monitoring and proactive attention. An occurrence of any event, alert, error, or unusual state can potentially lead to a down time of critical applications, leading to revenue leakage. A timely action before such an event can occur, is a great value addition to prevent revenue leakage.

- The IT operations often work in siloes. There may be situations when the IT application and infrastructure monitoring are not synchronized. The impact is high since the non-availability of one component is equivalent to the non-availability of both.

- CIOs are challenged to balance between the innovation and keeping the light on in the context of IT operations. The IT Operations teams are often overwhelmed by the humongous data generated by the disparate and diverse tools and often face burnout and demotivation. Talent retention becomes a major issue and as the resources move around in the enterprise or leave, the knowledge and experience that they take with them creates a void.

To address these challenges, there is a strong need to effectively make sense of the huge volumes of data generated by the various systems like monitoring, logs, network topology, tickets, and incidents, and to leverage it to the advantage of the enterprise to predict, monitor, and manage the events in the IT landscape is of immense value.

The purpose of AIOps is exactly to do that. AIOps works on the IT Operations' data generated from the plethora of tools, servers, applications, to generate insights and inferences. The data generated from these monitoring and event management tools, application, infrastructure logs, is of high volume, high veracity, and high variety, as well as complex. Due to this, the bulk of this data is often left unleveraged in enterprises since correlating this data to identify meaningful patterns at the enterprise scale would be an immense task. That is the place where AIOps comes into play. It tries to make sense of the data to predict the occurrences of various events in the IT ecosystem, notify the right stakeholder, and assist in resolution. The primary capabilities of AIOps thus include the following:

- Event detection
- Event localization
- Event remediation

Take a look at the following diagram to understand AIOps:

The adjoining figure depicts the capabilities of AIOPs and positions them in the context of enterprise IT Operations.

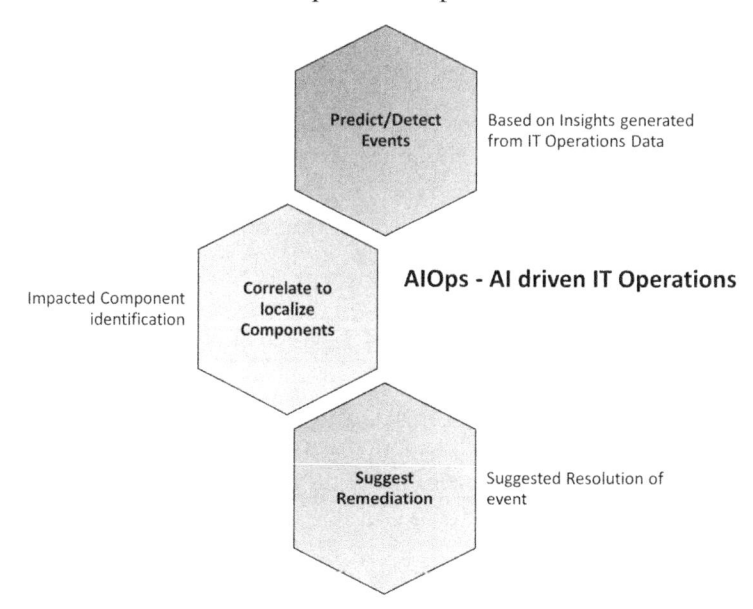

Figure 7.4: AIOps

Working of AIOps

Let us now understand how AIOps work. The primary resource that AIOps works on is data. As discussed, there are various data sources that generate a high volume of diverse data. These include the following:

- Alerts and events from monitoring systems
- Network topology data with nodes and deployment units
- Various types of logs – application, infrastructure, middleware, networking
- KPIs and metric dashboards
- Tickets and incident data
- Chats, transcripts, and other customer interaction data for issue resolution

As you can see, this is a mix of structured, unstructured, and semi-structured data.

AIOps has the machine learning models that can ingest these various types of data and can synthesize it to detect occurrences, and derive insights and recommendations about event occurrences, alert prevention, or issue resolution.

The primary functions of AIOps can thus, be enumerated as follows:

- Data ingestion
- Data correlation
- Pattern identification
- Insights generation
- Resolution recommendation

The following diagram (*figure 7.5*) will help you to understand the primary functions of AIOps:

> Data Ingestion → Data Correlation → Pattern Identification → Insights Generation → Resolution Recommendation

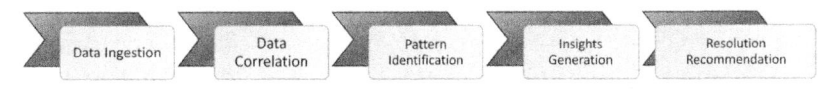

Figure 7.5: How AIOps Works

Let us now understand what happens in each of these functions, as follows:

- **Data Ingestion**: In this function, the heterogeneous data from the various types mentioned earlier from the cloud instances and on-premises ones are discovered and ingested. This data will then go through pre-processing, where it is usually cleansed to reduce the noise and normalize, if needed.

- **Data Correlation**: In this function, the machine learning algorithms along with the natural language processing algorithms work on the relevant unstructured, semi structured, and structured data to interpret the data and find any correlation between them. For example, whenever there is a new application released in a certain environment, say Test 1, a particular node hosting the associated database slows down and eventually crashes. The machine learning algorithms of AIOps identifies the correlational parameters and determines the correlation between them.

- **Pattern Identification**: In this function, the machine learning algorithms and the natural language processing algorithms identify the patterns in the data. It discovers which data elements are part of the "*cause*" and which are impacted as the "*effect*." It also detects any abnormal behavior in the system which is not part of the "*normal*" system operational behavior.

- **Insight generation**: Based on the preceding activities of event correlation and pattern generation, the system generates insights and inferences based on the machine learning algorithms. This could be insights like a specific system is predicted to have slow performance in the next two hours or detection of an issue of unstable behavior in a particular application node etc. These insights are usually accompanied with the identification of the impacted component – application, infrastructure nodes, networking nodes, etc. This helps in identifying and localizing the problem and guiding the users on the blast radius of the problem. Usually, a notification to the relevant user or user group follows. One of the common ways in which many AIOps systems notify the relevant users is throughChat Ops. This is the notification based on the different chat interfaces that is prevalent in the enterprise for an immediate connection with the engineers like MS Teams, Slack, and so on.

- **Resolution Recommendation**: The final activity is recommending the remediation actions based on the insights. The AIOps system can recommend the resolution actions and the next best action corresponding to the problem that is detected. It can do this based on the training and learning of the system and can refer to similar incidents that have happened in the past and bring up the resolution actions that were successful in resolving them.

Typically, the AIOps systems stop at recommending the resolution action, but there can be downstream automation to trigger the automated resolutions to remediate the issue, or hand over to a Site Reliability Engineer for further actions if not auto resolved. The resolution action cycle will pretty much follow what we discussed in the IT Operations Auto resolution use cases in *Chapter 5: Intelligent Automation Use cases*

What is important to understand is that these insights and the next best actions that are generated by the AIOps systems are not rule based or predefined. These are based on the ML models which are trained with *"calm"* and *"rough"* data to detect the problems and trained to recommend the remedial actions based on the nature of the problem. Most of the AIOps solutions and platforms in the market come with the pre-trained models that can be refined with the enterprise data to be ingested for training rapidly and be used to generate the insights real time.

The market has several players today focusing on AIOps. According to the analysts, there is a big market for AIOps and there are some key players who have built a significant capability around this, along with several contenders challenging the top players. AIOps is gaining a lot of importance in the CIO discussions and is becoming a priority area with many enterprises.

Before we end this topic, let us quickly touch upon some of the key players that are prevalent in the market today.

AIOps Platforms

The following table contains a list of some of the key players in the industry today who have come out with products and frameworks on AIOps; this is not an exhaustive list and as we speak, there are niche players and contenders coming up in this space rapidly:

Serial No	Platform/Tool	URL
1	AppDynamics	https://www.appdynamics.com/topics/what-is-ai-ops
2	bigpanda	https://www.bigpanda.io/
3	Bmc Helix	https://www.bmc.com/it-solutions/bmc-helix-operations-management.html
4	dynatrace	https://www.dynatrace.com

5	IBM AIOps	https://www.ibm.com/in-en/cloud/cloud-pak-for-watson-AIOps
6	Moogsoft	https://www.moogsoft.com/
7	Service Now AIOps	https://www.servicenow.com/products/it-operations-management.html
8	Splunk AIOps	https://www.splunk.com/en_us/it/AIOps.html

Table 7.3: Top AIOps Platforms for IT Operations

Future of work

I started to write this book during the Covid -19 pandemic, the first wave to be precise. The pandemic brought out the fragility of life. However, it has also brought about a host of positive opportunities all around us, in every industry and domain.

In our personal lives, we switched to *"work from home"* overnight. Our children started *"online learning"* overnight. The only thing that is constant is change. As we have seen during the entire year of 2020, throughout the pandemic, the way things worked around us changed. Businesses started adopting the new ways of work, changing their operating models to adopt to the new normal. As digitization became an absolute imperative, Intelligent Automation became the most important enabler. Most executives are now convinced that Intelligent Automation powered by AI is one of the key drivers that is shaping the future of work.

We started this book with the history of automation – how automation has been prevalent since ages and how IT automation in various forms and paradigms changed over the years and evolved. In the current times, automation enabled by AI or Intelligent Automation is taking interactions to a whole new level. This has started impacting the way men and machines are working together and will further impact how decisions are made, actions are triggered, and activities are executed. Let us discuss this in the final topic, Future of Work.

Dimensions of Future of Work

So, how does the future of work with Intelligent Automation look like?

If you think about work, there are three dimensions in any kind of work. The content of work itself, the workers, and the workplace. All these dimensions are impacted in some way or the other by Intelligent Automation and the pandemic has simply accelerated that change.

When talking about the content of work, we are seeing a sea of change. The routine, mundane repetitive tasks are no longer expected to be done by humans. With more and more back-office functions getting prioritized for Intelligent Automation, the following categories at work are becoming the prime candidates for Intelligent Automation:

- Back-office activities
- Mid-office data processing and decision making
- Administrative activities
- Front facing regular customer/business user interactions

As more and more of processes and activities around these areas get automated by using the different levers of RPA, AI, BPM, Integration, where will the workforce go? There is already significant apprehension around automation taking away the people's jobs. However, in our opinion, there will not be such drastic measures taken to let people go in such large numbers because of automation. What is going to happen is that the roles and skills of the resources will undergo a lot of change. The employees would have to unlearn their current job and learn newer things and newer skills.

The next dimension of the future of work is the workforce. Intelligent Automation will bring in a transition to a hybrid workforce where the digital workers like RPA bots, chatbots, and the other types of automation will have a significant play. There will be handoffs and interactions between the bots and humans. This will include decision making, recommending actions, and a lot of conversation. So, there is a strong need to plan and get the human workforce ready for such a change. The human workforce needs to understand, learn, and adopt to the man-machine collaboration as the enterprise transitions to the new hybrid workforce.

The third dimension to the future of work is the workplace. In my opinion, this dimension has gained tremendous importance as we traversed the pandemic. Hybrid workplace is a term which was almost unheard of a few years back, but that has a possibility of becoming a reality. It was COVID-19 and the lockdowns across the world, that made us realize that working from home or any other place is real, and can be managed with the right technology, tools, and enablement.

So, how will a typical workday look like? The activities and tasks that have a higher affinity to getting automated, and has a potential to generate business benefits will get automated. Intelligent Automation will not replace the human workers, but bots and human workers will coexist to run the business processes. The processes will become smart and need less human interventions. The human resources will spend less time on the routine activities, mundane back-office operations, and routine communications that are predictable. They will be engaged in those activities that machines are not capable of, like managing people, managing interactions and communications that are not routine, scenarios that need empathy, solving complex problems, and finding innovative solutions to problems. For example, instead of comparing the price of the parts from different vendors in a procurement process, humans will be engaged to negotiate the best price with the vendor. Intelligent Automation will add to the human intelligence and make them more efficient and intelligent. They will be engaged in areas where strong cognitive and emotional skills like logic and reasoning with empathy are necessary to function efficiently.

With such a significant change that's impending on the content of work, the enterprises need to prepare themselves and their workforce for such transformation. The drivers of the change need to be effectively communicated, so that the people, both the employees and the customers, are aware of the value of the change that is coming upon them and embrace the change with conviction. Otherwise, a set of disgruntled employees and customers can create a difficult workforce and negatively impact the balance sheets. In one scenario, as an example, a customer was calling her telecom service provider for a simple task execution like SIM activation, but wanted a clarification before she could trigger that task execution through the automated channels like the mobile app. However, to her frustration, after going through all the menus on the app as well as IVR, she was extremely disappointed to find that the human connect was no longer there. There was simply no option which said, *"Dial 9 for a customer service representative"*. Such situations can be very frustrating and the enterprises while embarking on Intelligent Automation at scale, need to create a balanced approach where the customer or employee experience is not compromised for the sake of automation. That is an area where there will be more and more collaboration between the humans and bots, so that the human touch is still there and the handoff between the humans and bots are perfectly orchestrated.

As we implement Intelligent Automation across the enterprise, we are essentially strengthening the human-machine collaboration through smart processes and intelligent workflows. However, what is important to understand here is that rebuilding the old, fragmented processes with newer technologies is not Intelligent Automation. We need to reimagine the processes, redesign the operating model with human-machine collaboration, and then optimize the workflows to make them intelligent and self-adapting.

The human workforce is and will still be critical in the age of Intelligent Automation. In our opinion, to ensure that we can operate and thrive in an environment of Intelligent Automation, the human workforce needs to come out of the traditional ways of doing work – be it the back office or the front office. The machines can be trained in various ways to do the tasks, and they can be trained to think and reason. But all of these is based on the learning we give them. They can consolidate the data, execute transaction, and even learn and recommend. So, what happens when you need to derive intelligence or insights intuitively? The machines do not have intuition, yet. So, logical reasoning, creative designing, critical thinking, and problem solving are some of the key skills that we need to focus on to thrive in the era of Intelligent Automation. Another important skill, which might sound a little philosophical is ethics and morale. As human beings, we possess and develop these values, and these are some of the key attributes that will continue to differentiate us in what machines can do and what the human force will contribute to the future of work.

The future of work is hybrid.

Conclusion

Now that we have understood the core concepts of Intelligent Automation and the latest trends around it, you are ready to get onto an engagement and practice what you have learnt in this book. This is an area that is evolving at a rapid pace both from a business and technological perspective. There are new products, solutions and tools that are coming up, and the Intelligent Automation paradigm and the capabilities it entails are showing signs of evolution. As the adoption of Intelligent Automation along with its constituent technology components increase and the maturity enhances, we will need to address a wider set of problems. For example, hybrid workforce is still being adopted and not yet prevalent at scale, and hence today we are defining a strategy and an operating model for the same. But when this becomes business-as-usual in the enterprise, we might need to address the issue of optimization of such a workforce. Such questions and many more will arise as newer and older technologies continue to converge to create Intelligent Automation in the enterprise. As the Greek philosopher Heraclitus said, *Change is the only constant* , we should be open and embrace the change consciously, adopting technology that benefits business, society and mankind as a whole.

References

You may refer to the following links for further information:

- https://www2.deloitte.com/us/en/insights/focus/technology-and-the-future-of-work.html
- https://www.ibm.com/thought-leadership/institute-business-value/report/automation-workflows
- https://www.myhrfuture.com/blog/2019/4/11/how-is-the-future-of-work-shaping-the-labour-market
- https://www.ibm.com/downloads/cas/7QGY1GDY
- https://www.hfsresearch.com/research/hfs-top-ten-process-intelligence-products-2020/
- https://www.gartner.com/en/information-technology/glossary/citizen-developer

Index

A

AI based automation
  non-technical characteristics 75, 76
  processes 73, 74
  technical characteristics 74
AI based automation, use cases
  about 77, 81
  customer behavior prediction 79
  financial services 77, 78
  IT operations 80
  optimized pricing 79
  retail 78
AI delivery life cycle
  about 81, 82
  data collection 83, 84
  dataset, building 83, 84
  deploying 85
  model, training 84
  refining 84
  testing 84
  use case identification and assessment 83
AI frameworks
  about 85, 87
  Deep Learning Framework 86
  Machine Learning Framework 86
AIOps
  about 183, 184
  functions 185
  platforms 187
  working 184, 185, 187

AI tools 85, 87
Artificial Intelligence (AI)
  about 7, 21, 22, 64, 114
  characteristics 23
  purpose, in automation 63
  types, in intelligent
    automation 64, 66
automated service request 126
automated service ticket
    creation
  about 126
  automation component 132
  detailed process 128
  high-level process 127
  high-level solution 129-131
  primary levers of automation,
    identifying 129
  secondary levers
    of automation,
    identifying 129
automated ticket resolution
  about 133
  automation
    component 138, 139
  detailed process 134, 135
  high-level process 134
  high-level solution 136-138
  solutions 139, 140
automation
  about 2, 3
  evolution, in information
    technology 3-8
  Automation Center of
    Excellence
  about 150
  functions 153, 154

need for 151-153
organizing 155
automation component
  about 122
  case creation
    automation, by API 122
  case creation
    automation, by RPA 122
  data, consolidating from
    external sources 124
  data, consolidating from
    internal sources 124
  data extraction, from image
    document 122-124
  data extraction, from PDF
    document 122-124
  risk assessment 124, 125
  single customer
    view, building 124
automation, stages
  about 8, 9
  activity 14-16
  basic automation 9, 10
  intelligent automation 12-14
  intermediate
    automation 10-12
  process 14-16
  tasks 14-16

B
Banking, use cases
  about 115, 116
  automated service request 126
  automated service
    ticket creation 126

automated ticket
    resolution 133
KYC processing 116
basic automation 9, 10
blockchain 28, 90-93
blockchain based automation
  immutability 93
  processes 93
  single source of truth 93
  traceable provenance 94
  trust 94
Business Intelligence 25, 26
Business Process
    Management 24

C
capital market 96
Center of Excellence (CoE)
  about 150
  setting up 166
Center of Excellence (CoE)
    models
  about 155, 156, 161, 162
  centralized CoE
      model 156, 157
  federated CoE model 157
  governance 165
  hybrid CoE model 157-160
  process 160
  technology 163, 164
centralized CoE model 155-157
Chatbots 27, 28
citizen development
  about 177
  overview 177-179
  platform, in intelligent
      automation 179-181

  problems 181, 182
  tools 182
collaborative filtering 71
content based filtering 71
Customer Due Diligence 118
Customer Management System
    (CRM) 173

D
deep learning 64
detailed process view
  about 118, 119
  automation
    components 122
  high-level solution
      diagram 121
  primary levers
    of automation, identifying 120
  secondary levers
    of automation, identifying 120
digital identity 95

E
Electronic Data
    Interchange (EDI) 5
Electronic Data
    Processing (EDP) 4
enterprise automation,
    challenges
  about 142-144
  absence of defined
      strategy 144, 145
  automation adoption
      resistance 146
  complex technology
      architecture 147
  operating model,
      limitation 146, 147

resources 147, 148
siloed automation across enterprise 145
unclear ROI 145, 146
Enterprise Resource Planning (ERP) 173

F
federated CoE model 156, 157
functions, AIOps
  data correlation 186
  data ingestion 185
  insight generation 186
  pattern identification 186
  resolution recommendation 186

H
hybrid CoE 156
hybrid CoE model 157-160

I
image recognition
  about 67, 68
  AI, benefits in automation 71, 72
  machine learning 71
  Natural Language Processing (NLP) 69, 70
  prediction system 70
  recommendation system 70, 71
Information Architecture (IA) 13
integration
  about 26, 27, 108, 109
  use cases 109-111

intelligent automation
  about 12-14
  AI, types 64, 66
  dimensions 188-191
  future 30, 31, 188
  impact 29, 30
  overview 148-150
  use cases 114, 115
intelligent automation, examples
  about 16, 18
  automated email processing 16
  automated invoice processing 17, 18
intelligent automation, technology components
  about 18, 19
  Artificial Intelligence (AI) 21, 22
  blockchain 28
  Business Intelligence 25, 26
  Business Process Management 24
  Chatbots 27, 28
  integration 26, 27
  Internet of Things (IoT) 28
  Robotic Process Automation 19, 20
  Virtual Assistants 27, 28
  workflow automation 24
intelligent automation, with blockchain use cases
  about 95
  digital identity 95, 96
  financial record keeping 97

financial services 96
inheritance 95, 96
logistics 97
intermediate automation 10-12
Internet of Things (IoT)
  about 28, 98
  characteristics 99
  connected devices 99
  data acquisition 100
  data processing 100
  data transfer 100
  scalability 100
  security 100
  sensing ability 99
  working 98
IoT based automation
    processes 102, 103
IoT based automation
    project 103-105
IoT implementation
  in intelligent automation 102
IoT use cases
  about 100-102

K
KYC processing
  about 116, 117
  detailed process view 118
  high-level process 117, 118

L
labor intensive 44

M
Machine Learning
  about 64
  reinforced learning 65

supervised learning 65
unsupervised learning 65

N
natural language
    interpretation 74
Natural Language Processing
    (NLP) 44, 69, 70
non disruptive 36
non-technical characteristics,
    AI based automation
  automatability 76
  benefits 77
  complexity 77

O
Optical Character
    Recognition (OCR) 44, 68

P
prediction system 70
process mining
  about 171, 172
  in intelligent
      automation 173-176
  primary objectives 174
  tools 176
programmable software 36

R
recommendation system 70, 71
reinforced learning 65
Robotic Process
    Automation (RPA)
  about 7, 19, 20, 114
  characteristics 20, 21, 35
  examples 20
  purpose 34

RPA API 56
RPA, benefits
  about 37
  audit trail 41
  consistency 40
  employee time savings 38
  human errors, avoiding 39
  improved process
    efficiency 38
  increased accuracy 39
  reliability 40, 41
  scalability 41
  strategic tasks 40
  turn around time 39, 40
RPA bot
  about 56
  attended bots 56
  hybrid or mixed bots 57
  unattended bots 56
RPA, characteristics
  non disruptive 36
  rule based 36
RPA delivery life cycle
  business case validation 53
  delivery planning 53
  environment
    preparation 53, 54
  use case identification
    and assessment 52, 53
RPA implementation
  about 54
  design and development 54
  monitor and measure 55
  testing and deployment 54, 55

RPA, practices 51, 52
RPA, processes
  about 42
  non-technical
    characteristics 44, 45
  technical characteristics 42-44
RPA products 56
RPA tools 56-58
RPA, use cases
  about 45
  core banking 46
  Customer Management 48
  finance and accounting 46
  financial crime 46
  generic use cases 49
  IT operation, use cases 50, 51
  Patient Management
    in Healthcare 48
  payroll in HR 49
  procurement 47, 48
  Vendor Management 48

S

smart contract 91
supervised learning 65

T

technical characteristics,
    AI based automation
  data availability 75
  image processing 75
  image recognition 75
  learning and inference 75
  natural language
    interpretation 74
  recommendation 75

U
unsupervised learning 65
User Interface (UI) 180

V
Virtual Assistants 27, 28

W
workflow automation
  about 24
  characteristics 25
workflow based automation
  about 105, 106
  process 106-108
World Economic
     Forum (WEF) 33

Printed in Great Britain
by Amazon